My Real-World Violin Shop

Practical Perspectives & Procedures

by Henry A. Strobel

It's the way I do it.
Maybe not your way
Or their way,
But it's OK.

BOOK TEN OF THE STROBEL SERIES FOR VIOLIN MAKERS:

Book One	*Useful Measurements for Violin Makers*
Book Two	*Violin Maker's Notebook*
Book Three	*Health of the Violin, Viola, and Cello*
Book Four	*Art & Method of the Violin Maker*
Book Five	*Violin Making, Step by Step*
Book Six	*Cello Making, Step by Step*
(Video) Seven	*"Watch Me Make a Cello, Step by Step"*
Book Eight	*Viola Making, Step by Step*
Book Nine	*Reflections (Personal Essays)*
Book Ten	*My Real-World Violin Shop*

See www.HenryStrobel.com for these and other books we publish.

Henry Strobel, Violin Maker & Publisher
Aumsville OR, 97325 USA

Copyright © 2003
Henry A. Strobel

Library of Congress Control Number 2003090764

ISBN 1-892210-03-7

Second Printing of the First Edition, June, 2005
Printed in the United States of America

For a complete descriptive catalog,
convenient secure online ordering,
lots of interesting information,
and fine photographs
visit our website:

www.HenryStrobel.com

Dedicated to inspiring string teachers
generously sharing their art,
growing young musicians,
letting beauty shine
and resound.

PREFACE TO THE FIRST EDITION

It's about time for another Strobel book. I wrote the last one almost five years ago. In the meantime I published a couple by others, but they weren't "me." What to write about? Well, - what do I know? What have I been doing (reasonably successfully and satisfactorily) for the past twenty years? Yes, operating what I call my "real-world" violin shop. At least this is the real world for me, my family, and my customers. There are different kinds of violin shops, maybe most are different, in different contexts, different "worlds" indeed, but my kind is sorely needed nearly everywhere. This book is to pass on what I have learned of this, from my own perspective, however nearsighted. I have been working mostly with students, practically and clearly in the public interest, not in a great gilded studio where wealth is aggressively created from the residue of the past, and with real world violins that fly on their own merits, not those acquired by association. My limited experience is told here "for what it is worth," of a country violin shop with good vibrations and happy customers.

real´-world´ the realm of practical or actual experience, as opposed to the abstract, theoretical, or idealized sphere of the classroom, laboratory, etc. . .

Random House Unabridged Dictionary

Countless readers of my other books have wondered, some in the mail, others out loud, whether it were possible or practical to turn their interest in violin making to a profit or a livelihood. These may be young people idealistically attracted to the beauty and mystery of the violin, or they may be mid-life craftsmen looking to turn their avocation of violin making into a new career. The former, if they graduate from one of the professional schools of violin making, will probably find work in some conventional violin shop, and may eventually succeed as independent artist makers. The latter, although they may have missed the boat for the violin school, given the ability, studying at summer sessions, part-time work, or the like, and assiduous self education (even with the Strobel books!), may succeed (and many have) in establishing themselves in small or home violin repair shops.

That is the stuff of this book. People all over need music more than ever. There are more beginning and continuing string players than ever, especially in the elementary schools. But economic conditions and budget limits make the availability and maintenance of decent, affordable instruments a challenge. It doesn't require expensive instruments. They need not come from or be serviced by a prestigious, expensive violin shop (who usually have bigger fish to fry anyway). It does require someone who will do it reasonably and right. This is humble work, requiring nevertheless the care and accuracy that a craftsman can be proud of. *(If you are not by nature and experience a craftsman, this is not for you.)*

You will need to be in varying proportions both craftsman and salesman. Being a shopkeeper is probably the last thing I would have sought to be (considering myself more along the lines of artist or philosopher). I still cannot see myself actually trying to *sell* someone something. If I like it and the customer likes it and we like each other and the price is attractive, it should sell itself. An unreliable theory to be sure, but it does reflect to a degree my experience, although I was perhaps more fortunate than some, landing in the Salem, Oregon area, which has long had a richly successful school string program. I was welcomed by the local schools, who were naturally pleased to have a resident violin maker to supplement the services of the music stores. They also encouraged me to independently offer instruments to the hundreds of fourth and fifth graders starting string instruction each year. This is a good way to acquire some long term customers, and since the instruments are traded back and reused time and again the return on investment can be good. But the real reward is in the shining faces of the little fiddlers, and in the contribution you make to the community.

Some within the trade will perhaps think I am promoting "malpractice" by encouraging readers who aren't graduate violin makers to do basic essential and affordable work on violins. Well, such work is already an inevitable fact and a necessity, and I am encouraging and enabling them to do it right, and to know and observe their limits! *This book is not only for the violin maker who is considering "hanging out his shingle,", but for those already launched and in need of navigational aids in these choppy waters.*

Here then is the basic plan presented in this book - and possibly your "plan."

> First learn by study, making, playing, repairing and adjusting your own violins. Only after you have the essential knowledge (and self-knowledge), skill, experience, and motivation, should you:

> Establish a repair business. You will gain further experience, customers, and contacts, including local schools, with little risk and cost. (Work on inexpensive student grade instruments only unless you are professionally qualified!)

> As part of the repair business you will stock replacement parts, strings, cases etc. The natural extension is to offer these to your customers, and you are now, in a small way, in "sales."

> You will naturally acquire and repair used instruments from time to time and this puts you at the threshold of sales in a larger way. You can stop right there with repairs, or you can add a whole new dimension to your business, renting and selling string outfits. But this has its pitfalls and complications, as well as its challenges and opportunities.

So we will speak first of *repair*, which is essential, and second of *sales*, which is a further option for the brave and expert. Of course we all have to provide *service*.

Please note that this book builds on the previous Strobel books for violin makers. It does not and could not repeat the material in them, which is why the coverage of some things here is incomplete. (And you should be conversant with the content of those other books before going into this business.) The repair procedures described here are merely supplements suited especially to the small commercial shop. At the back I have provided a table of contents of the Strobel books for an overview of where to find information on particular subjects. These little books are the most widely used of their kind, about 100,000 sold, and I hope this one as well will be both practical and interesting, despite its mundane subject matter.

Henry Strobel, Oregon, 2003

TABLE OF CONTENTS

Introductory

Preface 5

Perspective 8

Choices (Scope of the Business) 10

Repairs

Repairs 12

Sources of Equipment 17

Sources of Information 19

Selected Email Postings (Appendix I.) . . 20

String Check List Form 21

Adjusting a Violin (A Checklist) 22

Young Person's Guide 24

Repair Job Log Form 25

Common Repair Procedures 26

Labor Charges and Rates 31

Technical Update 35

Sample Shop Advertisement 37

Sales

Sales 38

Prices and Choices for Students 38

What's in a Name? 39

Seller and Buyer 42

Sources of Instruments, Etc. 44

The Public School Connection 47

Rental and Rent to Own 47

More on Pricing 50

Administrative

Office Procedures and Forms 52

Afterword 53

Sample Forms

Sales Receipt, Advertisement 54

Rent-to-Own Contract 55

Simple Rent Contract 56

Installment Contract 57

Evaluation Loan Contract 58

Sample Appraisal 59

More

Appendix I. Email Postings 60

Appendix II. (Reference Overview) Contents of the Strobel Books for Violin Makers . 77

PERSPECTIVE

"First, do no harm." (Hippocrates, "Father of Medicine," ca 400 BC, Greek physician)

"Know thyself." (Socrates, ca 450 BC, Athenian philosopher)

Let's be realistic. If you haven't already demonstrated your skill in making violins good enough to sell, you probably should not touch instruments that belong to other people. This doesn't mean you have to belong to the "union" (AFVBM, etc.). The vast majority of shop proprietors and violin makers do not. But you have to be a fine craftsman who knows string instruments, and who will not damage them. Sorry, but this often rules out the moonlighting string teacher. The violinist who really understands violins is a rarity. Reputation and competence go together. If you don't know what you're doing, it will show in loss of customers, unfortunately in some cases, not nearly soon enough. Your business (and it must be run like a business) is first and foremost a service. This is how you prove yourself worthy and attract and keep customers.

Children and schools do need affordable violin repairs, and as a result teachers, dads, and sundry tinkerers try to fill the breach. This is well meaning and occasionally successful, but every area has the hack who epoxies or bolts broken necks and "restores" instruments by stripping them - sometimes in lye! - and revarnishes them dreadfully. We can do a whole lot better than that and still not be good enough.

Oh, about violin making proper. We're not really talking about that here. If you want to do that full time and can establish your name, fine. Most violin makers, even trained professionals will be doing mostly repairs, sales, etc. in the boss's shop or their own. If you have your own "real world" violin shop serving the public, you're not going to be "whittling" all day. You'll spend a lot of time talking with other people, repairing and selling things that other people made, perhaps people in China who did carve and scrape all day, happy to have the job, becoming expert at it by rapid repetition, but most unlikely to become prima donnas about it. The competition is tough.

❧

In the hierarchy of music we have

> The Composition (composer)
> The Performance (musician)
> The Instrument (maker)

At the top is the music, the opus, or ideal. Second is the musician with a specific *re-presentation*, or interpretation. Only third is the instrument or *tool*. We are, as H. Allen Smith would say, "low man on the totem pole." That's what we're working on, the tool. But it's essential too. It has to work right, facilitate learning and music making, and place no gratuitous obstacles in the path. Ours is a lowly, worthy, exacting, necessary, insightful job; we're all trying to make the same thing, or make it right, perhaps excelling in small degrees, but hardly original. Is it art? In a way, yes.

Why am I doing this work? And why are you doing it (or want to do it)? Usually because we would like to combine an interest or skill with our life's work. There are two ways to value our work

> 1 - by it's intrinsic worth - the artist's or artisan's pride in a job well done.
> 2 - by what we are paid for it.

Certainly the first of these is the better and higher, and some will forego some of the second in the public interest. Such is the case of those generous luthiers who are giving their time in Cuba, Haiti, Palestine, Algeria, Columbia, Morocco, and South Africa repairing instruments and training local repairmen to offset the sad state of string repair in those areas. They have founded a non profit organization registered in Belgium called *Luthiers Sans Frontières* (Luthiers without Borders) with Dr. Paul Jacobs as president. Its mission is to provide repair services to musicians, orchestras and ensembles in areas where no local services are available, mainly in developing countries. There are representatives in the USA, UK and France. Your help, either financial or in tools, instruments or material, is most welcome. For further information -

LSF, 119 Chemin des Crolites
B-7800 Lanquesaint
Belgium
Tel: +32/(0)68.44.53.19 au +32(0)478/24.05.34
Email: lsfbe@yahoo.com

See also Carl Applebaum's story from Cuba in *Strings* magazine August/September 2002 or at www.stringsmagazine.com/issues/strings104/feature_cuba.html

Some of you who have achieved a secure position in life may also wish to donate a part of your time or material to help less fortunate young musicians in your own communities and schools. Older amateur makers in particular may find this a rewarding outlet. It's partly a public service, and part of your pay will be your satisfaction from the appreciation of students for whom you are a friend and a facilitator.

What other skills do you need? People and business skills that fit the scope of your business. Musical skills? It's not essential to be a good violinist, but you must be able to tune, to cleanly bow, play scales and *feel* and *hear*. I am no great violinist, but did learn to play as a youth, and for most of us that is what got us bent toward violin making. Working to standards of adjustment as in *Useful Measurements for Violin Makers* is the minimum, but you must be able to feel the action of the instrument and bow and know what sounds good to the artist. You will be adjusting bridges and posts every day, evaluating the results, acting as a human spectrum analyzer to optimize the tone and response. Eventually you should be able to roughly judge a violin by simply plucking the strings. This skill is sharpened through the years by attention and practice - it doesn't come all at once. Most lack the gift of absolute pitch, but it is easy enough to tune to an A 440 Hz fork, and then to the relative fifths. For the bass, it's convenient to use a clip-on electronic tuner, since the low fourths are more difficult to hear, unless you are handy with harmonics. My violinist son George has perfect pitch. It's impressive see how he can immediately tune anything in the shop with no external reference. Of course if you are dealing in violins you had better be able to test them while buying or demonstrate them while selling. Ability to play is relatively unimportant in much of building, repairing, and rehairing bows, however.

What is absolutely required of a good craftsman (or doctor or any professional) is that he remain a student. "Lifelong learning" is the catchword. True, one learns much from experience, thus the better violin repairers tend to be the older ones. But read everything you can. Take advantage of what others have learned. Stay in touch.

Subscribe to periodicals and acquire reference books (See **Sources of Information** on page 20). Learn to use the internet as a ready reference and to use email and forums to ask questions of your peers, how they solve problems that may be new to you. Please read the chapter, *Technical Update* (The State of Violin Making) on page 35 .

ح

CHOICES (SCOPE OF THE BUSINESS)

Repair only, or sales too? Sales is considered in another chapter, but repair is required whether or not you go on to sell. (In any case you will have to provide replacement parts, and if you do not provide as a minimum strings, cases, accessories, and at least some inexpensive bows and instruments you will drive your customers elsewhere.)

Bowed string instruments only, of course. "No man can serve two masters." Bowed and plucked strings are in different worlds, and I often think that their players are too. It is true that violin and guitar are well matched in performance together. Both my son George and my mentor in lutherie, Leon LaFosse, played both violin and guitar, but the making and repair techniques are very different. At least my real world violin shop will specialize in bowed instruments only! (In any case I am not qualified to write on fretted instrument repair.)

Bowed strings basically include the quartet - **violins, viola, and cello. Basses** are different and large, and are excluded in most fancy violin shops. But in a general string repair shop, especially if you do school repairs, you will want to include basses - unless you simply lack the space or energy to work on them.

Your world will be different than mine, and I understand it may not be practical for large commercial or big city violin shops, or shops with many employees to operate along these lines. They have exposures that the small shop does not, and the bottom line is of keen interest to the shareholders. Nevertheless, all must follow this spirit, if they are to be truly successful in the human sense.

Family business only, or a growing concern with **employees?** Indeed if you are successful as a family or retirement business, controlling its growth can be one of the problems. It's always difficult and dangerous to turn business away, but this is necessary if you're out of your depth,

or if you want to stay at a given level to fit your space, your family, your time, or to avoid the complications of employees. For example, we decided early on we wanted a controllable business, to live comfortably in the country, and to avoid hiring employees. We were fortunate, in that sometimes family members prove unsuitable or incompatible, but ours were well adapted, in particular Susan, a congenial and smart accountant, and my sons Henry Jr and now George, my partners. Had we wanted to move into the city and grow wildly, we probably could have, but why?

City, suburban, or even rural? Urban locations with walk-in business are very different from home operations. Costs and complications are multiplied. Zoning restrictions always have to be considered, but a small, inconspicuous business can usually be operated from one's home. Open hours or by appointment? From the outset I decided I did not want to be tied to a fixed schedule, and did not want to be surprised by walk-ins, or babysit lurkers or those with a day off who felt like casually "trying" violins. Time is precious, and asking customers to call first filters out a lot of the noise. This plus being out of town has other benefits. It insures a certain time lag between when the customer calls and when he arrives, giving us time to get whatever they are looking for tuned and ready to show, and giving me time to shave in case I have been up all night writing. (Being an artist as well as a businessman has its complications.) Having said that, the important thing is to be positive, inviting, and immediately accommodating in answering the phone.

A prime consideration in starting any business, or turning a hobby into a business is to realize that it will require investment and time to succeed, if indeed it does. The outlook is much better if you have already succeeded in a first career and are making change midway. It's far harder if you are under pressure, desperate to succeed. And don't start too late. Starting after retirement may be too late, especially if you still have a lot to learn. I was still in my mid forties when I made the change from a successful electronic engineering career, had some resources from earlier investments, and a long time avocation of violin making. (I also had the good fortune to begin writing on the subject, which certainly helped me learn it and later provided a buffer of income from book publishing to cover the slow times. Our small family business has been modestly successful, providing employment for us and our sons - and subsidy for a daughter still in graduate school.)

School Repairs is an area that is likely to provide accessible work in most areas that have a school string program, if you are competent and fast. It is not lucrative, since the schools have little money. This in fact is your entree, since in the beginning you will be willing to work for less. It is also a good opportunity to learn, and the quality of the work required need not be of the highest order, although it must be correct, conservative, and workmanlike. I did a fair amount of this work early on. Sometimes the instruments are in distressingly bad condition, having been repaired by generations of the variously qualified or not. This is humble work indeed, but a start - you are paying your dues and getting paid at the same time. For goodness sake, don't put your repair label in this stuff, or you'll get blamed for everything ever done to the instrument! Some small shops specialize in this work, traveling around collecting and delivering it. It peaks in the summer, in preparation for September. The larger shops are not interested in this work; their skilled labor is needed more for their own inventory and consignment repair and restoration. I don't solicit this work either, but if local teachers bring it in I don't say no. Repair work remains the "bread and butter" of most small shops.

Other School Connections include **Bidding** to provide string instruments and supplies, and rent or **rent-to-own** programs. These are considered in more detail in the Sales Chapter. An important and special section of sales is "rent-to-own," which can provide an essential service to students, and can even be "big business" in those areas fortunate to still have a thriving school string program, as we have here in Salem, Oregon. Be aware that it requires a long-term commitment and a lot of bookkeeping. Typical school string programs start in the fourth grade with a half size outfit, less frequently one quarter or three quarters. But do not even consider this unless you are prepared to provide expert, fast, repair service to the instruments you provide. Otherwise you will have the same drawbacks (delays, high costs, incompetence) as the general music store, which frequently falls flat in this area of service. - unless they are fortunate to have someone like you.

(In this connection there may be the possibility of working for a music store or as a repair contractor to one. I have had no experience of or any interest in this, but clearly this book would still be pertinent.)

REPAIRS

Do it right and do it fast. Right for the customer (because it's right), and fast for you (because you're running a business, and life's too short to waste).

Don't do more than is necessary. Fewer mistakes will be made, and fewer things will have to be undone or redone. Where practicable, what you do should be conservative and reversible, especially on valuable instruments.

Introduction

I came into the violin business as a second career. From my correspondence as a writer and publisher of books in this field, I know many others who have. Without the lifelong immersion in the training and atmosphere of the violin shop, and without the trade connections and correct cachet, however, they will not succeed as professional artist makers. To put it bluntly most will be unable to compete even with the high quality work mass produced in emerging countries. There are exceptions, and I may claim to be one. While my own business has run to professional artistic making and repairing (and of course to writing and publishing), the bulk of it has been the operation of my "real world" violin shop, the majority of our customers being teachers and young students. Of those who read my books there will be many peaceful amateurs, but a few will be driven to master this craft, to make a living of it as a sound and satisfying second career, and to be socially responsible as well.

To some of these mature violin makers, I say, "Why not provide a service to local students?" But you must be careful and competent - how you get to that point may vary, but you need to be a natural, proven craftsman, honest, hard working and hard studying, and of course a self-starter (or you wouldn't be a violin maker or a businessman). Professional school, classes and workshops, working in a violin shop, books all help. High standards are a must. Knowing and abiding within your limits is another.

But it does need to be said that too often someone unqualified steps into repair work and may not even realize what a terrible job he is doing. I shudder when such work is brought in by a customer whom I cannot or will not turn away. Ruefully I realize that I will probably dull my chisel cleaning out the bow mortises full of glue and the wire used by the well meaning but ill-advised repairman in place of the practical, traditional thread. I will have to make replacement plugs. Or try several solvents before I

succeed in removing the mystery glue that let the fingerboard sink down. A repairman whom I don't know, but whose work I recognize fits every bridge with the back tip angle exactly reversed. Plastic wood has its place, but not daubed on to replace expanses of missing edges. Another "restores" scratched up instruments by covering them with a heavily pigmented brown "varnish." Or, alternately, spraying on a coat of shiny clear stuff, the better perhaps of the two evils.

Yes, I understand that many graduate professional makers in the trade will object to those without similar credentials setting themselves up in business. But the reality is that they are not going to do this kind of work themselves, at least at rates that many schools and students can afford. Nor indeed does much of the work on inexpensive student instruments require the same high level. It is easy to say, as it often is by the tonier shops that there is only one way to do a job - the right way. But this maxim stands up to scrutiny no better than the other that we hear so frequently, "you get what you pay for." In fact there are different right ways to do a given repair, depending on the grade and use of an instrument.

For *example*, consider an inexpensive small school cello that has sustained a back sound post crack. Doing this the "right" way with a plaster cast and inlaid patch would cost much more than the cello. But the ingenious repairman can apply a large 2-3 mm thick cross-grain maple cleat that, clamped to conform to the back curvature, provides the strength and a little tension to hold the crack closed, and a secure platform for the (slightly shortened) post to sit on. This is a reversible, easy repair, with normally negligible acoustic drawbacks at this level. If one is really good, perhaps he could install this without removing the front! Well, no, that would not be advisable, but the skilled repairman should be able to open and close a school cello in half an hour. (Unless it was built with that horrible glue that requires a saw to open it!)

Shop Layout

I may not be the best one to advise on this, since my own shop arrangement developed over many years without a real plan. Most will not have an optimum layout in the beginning; it's more important to have the work. I am going to assume that your small shop will be in or adjoining your home, and there are no zoning problems. This should be true if you are only making or repairing and have visitors by appointment only. Being in a rural area we have little concern about neighbors, but if you are in suburbia you need to resolve in advance questions about zoning, parking, signs, noise, etc. Open door walk-in traffic will definitely be out. A roomy, well lighted workshop area is necessary. While it's convenient to have everything together, you will want some separation of functions (and to keep the sawdust out of the varnish, etc). If you are doing only repairs this workshop will be enough, provided it has windows, a sink, suitable workbenches, shelves, and an outside door (unless your wife enjoys having customers wandering through the house). If you are doing sales to any extent you will need a pleasant room for customers to see and try instruments, i.e. a showroom or "store." I ended up with several areas, added as needed, starting with a tidy inside room for violin and bow work, then walled off half the two car garage for cello building and repair, and later added a well insulated, air conditioned sales room onto the house. Spare bedrooms and some barn space are used from time to time for overflow storage of instruments, books, tools, and wood. (I also have a large library upstairs for research, writing, and publishing.) The down side to all this distributed space is inefficiency - the up side is all the exercise I (we) get running back and forth between these areas.

Specific Repair Areas

See also *Violin Making Step by Step, Our Work Space, pages 8-9* Solid, flat, workbenches as needed are secured to the wall and floor in front of windows fitted with venetian blinds for light control. Next time I will have at least one bench away from a wall for access from all sides. This is desirable also for working with or teaching with a left-handed person (like Henry Jr). While left-handed violinists all conform to convention, this can hardly be expected of craftsmen and may require adaptation of bow

rehairing fixtures and the like. Of course both fluorescent and adjustable (swing arm or gooseneck) lighting and a sink with hot and cold water. Frequently used hand tools are kept ready to hand in racks designed for them at or near the benches. Parts and materials are stored on shelves or in appropriate drawers. I like to use the oak cabinets of drawers that became available from libraries when card files were replaced by computer terminals.

The old saw of my father,"A place for everything, everything in its place." is never more true than in a violin shop. This is true for both tools and materials. Tools must be kept clean, sharp, and immediately accessible. We don't need a lot of tools, but we need the essentials. *The violin maker is also a toolmaker.* Some tools are simply not available, cost too much, or are needed faster than we can get them otherwise. For example, we will need bridge templates for all the sizes of instruments that we service. We simply cannot fit bridges quickly and accurately without them. See *Useful Measurements for Violin Makers* for full size templates, pages 12, 18.

When used, stationary power tools in the converted garage area can be connected, when used, to a shop vacuum cleaner. They really are not used enough to justify a major dust control system. The remaining half of the garage is still used as (surprise) a garage, but the overhead door makes this a convenient receiving area for unpacking arriving shipments of supplies and instruments, especially cellos and basses.

Whether in a repair or sales area, we need safe convenient places to put the instruments. In our sample illustrated advertisement in the Sales Chapter, page 37, you can see several methods:

Violins and violas are hung by the scroll on square U-shaped bailing wire hangers, inserted through holes in a support strip before screwing it to the ceiling. These hangers are 2.5 inches wide, spaced at 6 inch intervals. If you used these for cellos, as I do in the repair area, they would be 4 inches wide and spaced as needed. (No sagging "clothes lines," please!)

Cellos can be displayed in box-like stands, but I prefer floor racks where they can lean against a wall and are conveniently accessible.

Basses are awkward, but can be hung against the wall using the strong plastic-padded steel hooks such as are used for bicycles. If basses or cellos are placed on their side on an uncarpeted floor, the bag should be on.

In the same photo is a dual purpose **sales counter**. After sawing out the top surface and installing well-supported 1/4 inch (6 mm) plate glass, I have a "mini-museum" for curious and valuable violins. (Don't let the kids climb up on this!)

Better bows are stored in the usual flat cases holding twelve each. Inexpensive student and rental bow are hung on L-shaped brass hooks spaced 1.5 inches apart. Note that they are hung inside the clear plastic bags they come in so they are not exposed to dust, etc.

Tools in General

Since you are already a violin maker, we can assume you already have most of the tools required. Perhaps you made only violins and violas. In this case you will need larger calipers and a multitude of larger clamps (which you can acquire as needed) suitable for working on cellos and basses. Some of the larger clamping and supporting fixtures, for example to apply an inlaid sound post in a bass, are best fabricated on the spot.

Spare and Repair Parts

Inventory is necessarily a compromise, and inventory control (especially if you also sell things) is critical. Best be conservative in starting out, adding categories as needed. Inventory can be kept low if you only buy things as needed, but this will cause every repair to have a longer turn around time, will require many small orders with larger shipping and bookkeeping overhead, and you will have lots of jobs in process at the same time distracting you and getting in your way. Making the customer wait is bad for you too.

Be sure to develop a good relationship with one good supplier who is reasonably close geographically, and whom you can phone and get intelligent service and same day shipping. For example here on the West Coast I have used Vitali Imports for decades; if

I were in the Midwest or East I would use someone else. I am speaking here of routine spare parts. For big-ticket things such as instrument, bow, and case inventory you will have to shop among several other specialist suppliers or manufacturers - who will conversely probably not be very good at supplying routine spare parts.

Strings, of course. Keep an ample supply of at least medium gauge and quality strings in steel and synthetic core, and a small supply of expensive gut strings for those few who need them. Avoid the straight strings in tubes. Straight storage is not really necessary. True, you don't have to unwrap them, but they are harder to organize and store, and you need strings in the square envelopes to sell anyway. I stock them all like this. You basically need strings for all the sizes and kinds of instruments you service, but at least token quantities for the others in case of customer emergency. Only very large shops can afford to keep all gauges and brands. Learn how to substitute brands.

But note: Use the right size! In emergencies you may substitute one size higher, but don't become known as the shop that cuts down full size strings for half size instruments - or worse, winds all the extra

"Looks like we're getting low again!"

length into the pegbox! Strings don't work that way.

Bridges - Like strings, a stock of all the common sizes in medium grades are the minimum to keep on hand. You will not, in a small shop, be able to keep all the styles, grades, widths, and heights. Some you will need to special order. But keep at least some different viola widths, and some of the high quality bridges for the better instruments and advanced or professional musicians.

But note: Always use "real" bridges, properly fitted to the instrument, not the soft white cheap ones, and definitely not the "one size fits all" type with the ball joint feet. These are not necessarily bad, and the upper edge can be adjusted, but they are a makeshift for music stores, not for the professional violin shop. For better instruments use the better grades of treated *Aubert* or *Despiau* bridges.

Sound post stock. As new instruments age they will need slightly longer posts. Keep a supply for violin, viola, cello, and bass in typical diameters. You will also have to replace lots of awful posts.

Shoulder rests, Kun original in all sizes, others to taste.

Cello endpin stops and straps.

Chinrests smooth lightweight black matte plastic or wood in at least three styles. Low "teka" and "edu" and "Flesch" (centrally placed). Others optional to taste and fit.

Other General Supplies

Plain good ebony **pegs** and **endbuttons** in all sizes and a few in boxwood and rosewood for matching individual replacements. The fancy ones can be special-ordered as needed.

Same for **tailpieces,** except that for small student instruments the lightweight metal type with integrated fine tuners is recommended. For better and full size cellos, the similar looking fiberglass ones, e.g. Wittner type, are good. You will also need dozens of Wittner type "stable" **fine tuners,** preferably in the black finish, in two sizes for violins (one for 4/4 and 3/4, and one for 1/2, 1/4, and 1/8), one for violas, and two for cellos (one for 4/4, 3/4, and another for 1/2 and smaller).

Cello endpins are needed frequently for replacement. There is a general trend to use longer endpins nowadays, and many school instruments still have short ones. They are also frequently damaged or bent. For some reason many of the cheap imported cellos have poorly fitted endpin plugs, as if the maker could not afford an endpin reamer and used a rat-tail file freehand. They are commonly very loose, whether from poor fitting or shrinkage of the wood plug.

Wolf eliminators for cellos. Both "tube" and "resonator" types. See *Useful Measurements for Violin Makers* page 24.

Sacconi type **black nylon tailgut adjusters** in all sizes.

Spirit varnish and **colors** for repair and "touch-up," and good **hot hide glue.** See pages 27-39 of *Violin Maker's Notebook.*

Alcohol, denatured ethyl for cleaning bows and fingerboards and thinning spirit varnish.

Acetone for cleaning brushes and removing cyanoacrylate glue. Caution: it removes varnish!

Rubbing compound Meguiar's No. 4 (from the automotive store) for instruments and bows. Use conservatively.

Felt pads, 6mm thick for the rubbing compound. McMaster-Carr catalog no. 8334K32 white wool felt 1/4 in thick, 12 x12 in.

Walnut Oil, or linseed, as lubricant on spirit varnish on cloth "rubber" in French polishing.

Vinegar helps to remove "white" glue

Turpentine "pure spirits of gum turpentine," for thinning oil varnish, cleaning large rosin accumulations from the front of basses, etc.

Simple Green is a common commercial non-abrasive cleaning solution excellent for instruments and bows. It removes rosin, dirt, etc. and is considered quite safe to people and varnish.

I have also used *Citristrip Wipe Away,* which has a pleasant orange smell, to very easily remove rosin buildup from the fronts of lacquered school basses. Be sure to test all such things for safety to varnish before using!

Note: Before working with any of these solvents, etc. Please read the *Shop Safety* **chapter in** *Violin Maker's Notebook.* **They may readily penetrate the skin,** have toxic fumes requiring ventilation (for example from evaporation from a large surface, as the front of a bass!), or damage the eyes from splashes.

Peg compound, Hills' is still best, I think.

"Peg Drops," for use by teachers sparingly in an emergency to stop pegs from slipping. Sometimes helpful also to stop student bridges from sliding on lacquered instruments.

Polish/cleaner White "creme" type, that leaves a lasting luster. Avoid those oily concoctions - you know the kind. It comes in liter bottles for shop use or small glass bottles for customers. From Hammerl or Vitali, for example.

Cleaning cloths, untreated flannel, not for polishing or shop use, but optionally complimentary with sale or repair of instrument.

Beeswax excellent dry lubricant for tools, bow screws, and fine tuners.

Bow Repair Supplies

Hair, Long unbleached high quality white stallion for all bows except bass. Use black hair for this, which can be shorter and less expensive.

Cyanoacrylate ("crazy" type glue) for bow repairs. See www.loctite.com
411 clear thickened cyanoacrylate
410 black thickened cyanoacrylate Fills gaps in ebony.
(Loctite *Quicktite* is widely available in a convenient 5g container that doesn't easily clog.)

XNMS solvent (nitromethane). Reasonably safe to remove cyanoacrylate from varnish - test first.

Rosin, at least three kinds for violin/viola, cello, and bass. E.g. Hidersine. Round cakes only, please.

Rosin, powdered, to start unrosined bows.

Black leather for bow grips. Assorted.

Artificial whalebone wrapping. Also **silver wire.**

A **thin phenolic sheet** is an alternative to veneer for splining bows, e.g. McMaster-Carr no. 8525K411, 1/32 in thick, tan.

SOURCES OF EQUIPMENT

Note: The sources listed below are only a few *examples* out of many. *The presence of a source here in no way represents an unqualified endorsement, nor does its absence imply anything undesirable.*

Tool Sources

Frank Mittermeier Inc. (fine carving tools)
PO Box 2 Bronx, New York USA 10465
(800)-360-3843, fax (718)-518-7233
www.dastrausa.com

McMaster-Carr Supply Co. (all industrial tools, materials)
PO Box 54960
Los Angeles, CA 90054-0960
(562) 692-5911, fax (562)-695-2323
www.mcmaster.com

MSC Industrial Supply Co. (machine, electronic, tools, materials)
75 Maxess Road
Melville NY 11747-3151
(800) 645-7270, fax (800) 255-5067
www.mscdirect.com

Dick GmbH (*Fine Tools* catalog)
Donaustr. 51
94526 Metten, Germany
49 991 910930, fax 49 991 910950
www.dick-gmbh.de

Woodcraft (tools)
560 Airport Industrial Park PO Box 1686
Parkersburg WV 26102
(800) 225- 1153
www.woodcraft.com

General Violin Shop Supplies

Note: Most of these companies have free beautifully printed large color catalogs that are an education in themselves.

Dick GmbH (*Products for Musical Instruments* catalog)
Donaustr. 51
94526 Metten Germany
49 991 910930, fax 49 991 910950
www.dick-gmbh.de

Howard Core & Co. Inc.
PO Box 1650
Anniston AL 36207 USA
(800) 633-2302, fax (256) 238-8465
www.howardcore.com

International Violin Co Ltd

Clarkview Road, Suite 118
Baltimore MD 21209 USA
(800) 542-3538, fax (410) 832-2528
www.internationalviolin.com

S.V.S Tonewoods (beautiful complete catalog)
PO Box 54
840 00 Bratislava 4, Slovakia
421 903 464 124, fax 421 2 6531 3069
www.tonewood.sk

Vitali Import Company Inc.
PO Box 4218
Whittier CA 90607
(800) 325-8154, fax (562) 698-2429

Some Specialized Suppliers

(Many of these things can also be got conveniently from the general suppliers above.)

Bow Works (bow making supplies)
PO Box 263
Little River CA 95456
(707) 937-0570, fax (707) 937-248
www.bowworks.com

Hammerl GmbH & Co. KG (varnishes, etc.)
Hauptstraße 18
D- 91083 Baiersdorf, Germany
09133/2330 fax 09133/5171
www.hammerl.com

Kremer Pigments Inc.(varnish components)
228 Elizabeth St.
New York NY 10012
(800) 995-5501, fax (212) 219-2395
www.kremer-pigmente.com

Milligan and Higgins (315 gram high clarity hide glue)
Maple Avenue - P.O. Box 506
Johnstown, NY 12095
518-762-4638, fax 518-762-7039.
www.milligan1868.com

Northern Renaissance Instruments (early instruments, strings, varnish, information)
6 Needham Avenue, Chorlton-cum-Hardy
Manchester M21 8AA, U.K.
+44 (0) 161 881 8134, fax same
www.nrinstruments.demon.co.uk

You won't need tonewood unless you're a maker, but . . .

Orcas Island Tonewoods
679 Roehl's Hill Rd.
Olga WA 98279
(360) 376-2747, fax (360) 376-4080
www.rockisland.com/~tonewoods

John Tepper
PO 430
Shady Cove
Oregon 97539
1-541-878-3156
tonewood@internetcds.com

Northern Tonewood Company
PO Box 1505
42 Cooper Crescent
Goose Bay
Newfoundland & Labrador
Canada, A0P1E0
(709)896-3086 fax (709)896-0471
http://hvgb.net/~tonewood/

Sources of Wholesale Finished Instruments

This is a difficult, sensitive, competitive, changing area,
and I finally decided not to list my favorite vendors here.
I do not want to get into a conflict of interest or to
alienate any company. Also it is a highly competitive,
changing area, and I tend to alternate among several
suppliers as their quality and price varies. The quality of
these "commodities" is apt to vary with the current source,
and how stable their craftsmen, recipes, and quality
controls are. Keep in touch with a range of suppliers or
you may get left behind. Your flexibility as a small
company can give you an advantage over larger
competitors. I have not listed separate sources for cases
and bows above, which are available from the general
violin shop suppliers at similar prices, and will more likely
fit and cost less to ship if you buy them where you buy the
instruments. There is further advice and explanation in
the **Sales Chapter**.

SOURCES OF INFORMATION

Periodicals

These are good. Take advantage of your free business listing in the *Directory* and *Guide*. Their regular advertising is expensive. (Better to use your yellow pages and web site.)

The Strad, and its *Annual Directory* (for makers, players, dealers, etc. Excellent full size color posters of classic instruments with working measurements)
Orpheus Publications Ltd
SMG Magazines Ltd
3 Waterhouse Square
138-142 Holborn
London EC1N 2NY
UK
+44 (0)141 302 7744, fax +44 (0)141 302 7799
www.thestrad.com

Strings, and its *Annual Buyer's Guide* (for makers, players, dealers, etc.)
Strings Magazine
PO Box 767
San Anselmo, CA 94979
(415) 485-6946, fax (415) 485-0831
www.stringsmagazine.com

Books

Weisshaar, Hans, and Shipman, Margaret: *Violin Restoration, A Manual for Violin Makers*, Weisshaar-Shipman, Los Angeles, 1988

There are countless expensive photo books on violins, but few practical ones on repair (except of course mine).

Associations

These are all actually international but some have a localized focus. Starting with the first, coincidentally, I really must praise the MVA. Under the long leadership of David Brownell it has provided high quality technical information to its well integrated professional and amateur membership. It's Directory of Services for Violin Makers, published jointly with the SCAVM is itself nearly worth the cost of membership. These associations all have monthly or quarterly newsletters or journals, the most polished and prestigious, although not the most useful practically, is the VSA Journal. Most of these associations also hold conventions, meetings, and instrument making competitions, which can be very valuable and instructive.

Michigan Violin Makers Association (MVA)
Y. Y. Shum, 710 Green Road
Ann Arbor MI 39105
(734) 663-5919
t_mva@altvista.com

Southern Calif. Association of Violin Makers (SCAVM)
1113 Big Oak Ranch Road
Fallbrook CA 92028 USA
(760) 723-9548
www.scavm.com

Violin Makers of Arizona International (VMAAI)
Duree Shiverick
420 N. 2nd St.
Eagle ID 83616
(208) 939-9166
www.vmaai.com/membership.htm

The Violin Society of America (VSA)
48 Academy Street
Poughkeepsie, NY 12601 USA
(845) 452-7557, fax (845) 452-7618
www.vsa.to/membership.htm

Schools

I have only listed one of the full course professional schools here*, since they are not normally an option for the working repairman.

Oberlin Stringed Instrument Restoration Workshop
Conservatory of Music, Oberlin College
Oberlin OH 44074
(440) 775-8044, fax (440) 775-8942
www.oberlin.edu

National Music Museum (not a school)
The University of South Dakota
414 East Clark Street
Vermillion SD 57069
(605) 677-5306, fax (605) 677-5073

www.usd.edu
Violin Craftsmanship Institute
University of New Hampshire
Brook House, 24 Rosemary Lane
Durham, NH 03824 USA
(603) 862-4234, fax (603) 862-1113
www.learn.unh.edu/violin

Violin Making School of America *
308 East 200 South
Salt Lake City, UT 84111 USA
(801) 364-3651, fax (801) 364-3652
www.prierviolins.com

The Internet

This, specifically the "world wide web" has become a practically indispensable source of information in any endeavor, once you acquire the knack of judiciously choosing keywords for searching. For now *Google* is the best search engine, practically the only one I use. Most of the sources listed above have web sites, which also provide email addresses for questions, etc. You can find or find out anything fast, you can communicate quickly with the right people, further your education, or even conduct business.

Selected Email Postings

Email has taken over as the preferred and fastest way for individuals and businesses to communicate. Naturally I use it a lot in the publishing business, and of course I get a lot of questions (nearly daily) from those who use my books. In addition to that I have been a member of an international group of violin makers on the internet who exchange email, asking questions and presenting and discussing matters of interest (usually) daily since the beginning of 1995. Letting all the mail from this group pile up in my computer has filled a searchable mailbox of a hundred megabytes or so.

These violin makers are connected by a "list server," with a private, controlled membership (not to be confused with noisy public "newsgroups"). Members include top professionals as well as amateurs. It is limited to serious violin or bow makers by invitation.

Of course this correspondence is all private and copyrighted by the individual contributing members, but I carefully contributed some of it, which is copyrighted to me, and I reckon some of that is worth repeating here, and it will get me an easy extra chapter, so long as I don't quote anyone else. This is necessarily one-sided and uneven, but includes a lot of information and commentary on exactly the topics being covered in this book. The correspondence reprinted here is all "real" and worth further dissemination. I first wondered about including it, but I think you will find it interesting and educational, however unorganized.

See Appendix I. Selected Email Postings on page 57. If you would like to be invited onto the list, ask a member - me, for example. *But please remember that the purpose of this group is the advancement and sharing of the art and science of violin making (and of course repair), not of sales or dealing. Strictly technical, non-commercial.*

Minimum Inventory Checklist- Standard Strings

Instrument	String	Prelude	Helicore	Dominant	Larsen	Eudoxa	Corelli	Flexocore
4/4 Violin (Medium tension or gauge)	E	3 __	12 __	12 __		6 __		
	A	3 __	12 __	12 __		6 __		
	D	3 __	12 __	12 __		6 __		
	G	3 __	12 __	12 __		6 __		
4/4 Viola (Medium tension and length, others are special order)	A	2 __	12 __	12 __	6 __	3 __		
	D	2 __	12 __	12 __		3 __		
	G	2 __	12 __	12 __		3 __		
	C	2 __	12 __	12 __		3 __		
4/4 Cello (Medium tension, others special order)	A	6 __	6 __		6 __			
	D	3 __	6 __		6 __			
	G	3 __	6 __					
	C	3 __	6 __					
3/4 Bass (Medium tension, high tension and solo, etc. special order)	G		1 __				3 __	2 __
	D		1 __				3 __	2 __
	A		1 __				3 __	2 __
	E		1 __				3 __	2 __

Size		3/4	1/2	1/4	1/8	1/16	1/32	
Small Violin or Viola (Prelude medium)	E	6 __	6 __	3 __	3 __	2 __	1 __	
	A	6 __	6 __	3 __	3 __	2 __	1 __	
	D	6 __	6 __	3 __	3 __	2 __	1 __	
	G	6 __	6 __	3 __	3 __	2 __	1 __	
	C	3 __	3 __	3 __				
Small Cello (Prelude Medium)	A	6 __	6 __	3 __				
	D	6 __	6 __	3 __				
	G	6 __	6 __	3 __				
	C	6 __	6 __	3 __				
Small Bass (Corelli or Prelude, medium or strong)	G		2 __	1 __				
	D		2 __	1 __				
	A		2 __	1 __				
	E		2 __	1 __				

An example only. Your needs will vary. Physically inventory your strings regularly and check which to reorder. Order 3, 6, or a dozen or more at a time depending on usage rate. You may also want heavier or lighter strings to optimize tone or playability. E.g. a smaller ("short scale") viola may need a heavier (higher tension) string, and vice versa for a larger viola. In theory, the string stock will show in your accounting inventory, but in fact we are always pulling out strings to fit up new instruments, etc., and will run short unless we physically check from time to time.

ADJUSTING A VIOLIN (A Checklist)

(Note: This first appeared on my website. It is a simplified checklist, and of course does not include all the things that might need correction, nor the myriad potential factors of tone adjustment. It does certainly hit the high spots, however.)

ੴ

This checklist will help in one of the most typical, essential, and frequent tasks in the violin shop. That is "setting-up" or adjusting a violin for sound and playability. Here at Strobels' we definitely live in the real world, and a majority of the violins we supply are inexpensive new instruments for students. Even though new violins are purchased as "shop adjusted", this is often a matter of interpretation - or euphemism. Optimal adjustment for the student means he will not be faced with gratuitous obstacles. Of course nothing less than the best is tolerable for the professional.

Optimizing the adjustment is a matter of experience and sensitivity of touch and hearing, but we have learned from time and tradition certain good typical measurements. This is why I wrote *Useful Measurements for Violin Makers, A Reference for Shop Use*. It includes size and adjustment information for all sizes of the violin, viola, cello, and bass, and is indispensable for most violin shops, responsible music stores, and many professional string teachers.

So why am I writing this "checklist?" The idea just occurred to me this morning as I was working with my son, Henry Jr, who is learning the trade and setting up new student violins in our shop. Perhaps it will help others in similar learning situations. This is only an outline for a full size violin; the book has much more detail.

ੴ

● EXAMINE the violin overall. Note what needs to be **replaced**, or is missing. For example, we may decide to replace the original equipment strings with Helicore, the fine tuners with black Wittners, and the tailgut with a "Sacconi." See "Useful Measurements for Violin Makers," pages 19-21 for information on choosing and installing strings. If the bridge is a poorly cut, mushy one, we will choose and fit a hard one, a genuine Aubert or similar. Collect the materials needed.

● REMOVE the strings, bridge, tailpiece, chinrest, endpin, and soundpost. Leave the pegs in for now to avoid interchanging them.

(NOTE: The order of the next three steps may have to be altered. For example, a nut may have to be removed so a fingerboard can be properly planed.)

● Check the FINGERBOARD for the curvature and lengthwise concavity ("scoop") and correct it if necessary. This is often overlooked on student violins and causes no end of buzzes and botheration. A straight board is nearly tolerable, especially in the lower positions, but one that droops toward the bridge is not. Such a warp may occur when an instrument is shipped with the strings down tight against (instead of alongside) the fingerboard, or is packed too tightly. Also lift up on the lower end of the fingerboard to check if it is loose. This hidden problem is a frequent cause of neck warping.

● Check the fingerboard PROJECTION at the bridge line (between the inner soundhole notches), about 27 mm high on a normal 4/4 violin. If it is too low you may decide to "reset" it by loosening the upper half of the front, placing a shim between the base of the neck and the front, and regluing. (In more extreme cases, reject the violin - it was made wrong.)

● Check and correct the string NUT as necessary. They are generally too high on new factory fiddles, making them hard to play. File the nut down to about a mm above the fingerboard, and sloping down into the pegbox. Recut the grooves as needed about 5.5 mm string center to center, but all the grooves should be shifted about a mm toward the bass side. See the template in *Useful Measurements*, page 12. The string grooves at the nut (and at the bridge) should be about as wide as the string diameter, but only about 1/3 as deep. Use a "mouse tail" file. The string should rest "on," not "in" the grooves. Remove any sharp edges from the ends of the nut with a flat file, rounding them smoothly down to the fingerboard and pegbox. (On old violins the strings may be too low at the nut, causing buzzing. Make a new nut or place a shim (stain it black) under the old one so there is at least a quarter mm under the E string and a third of the string diameter under the others.)

● Make sure the PEGS fit and operate smoothly and securely after applying Hills' peg compound. Pegs on new violins often fit poorly, are too long, are out of round from shrinking, have ugly sawn ends, have too small or wrongly placed string holes, etc. See "Violin Making, Step by Step," pages 62-64 for details of peg fitting.

● Check the POST for correct grain direction, angle and fit of the front and back ends, and length. A too tight (too long) post can cause disastrous cracks as well as a cramped tone. See *Useful Measurements*, page 23 for its position and adjustment. Reset it through the treble soundhole, then looking through the endpin hole to check that it is vertical. Also note: a good rule is that the post should be about as far from the bridge as the front is thick. This helps keep thin violins from tubbiness and thick ones from brassiness.

● Install the FINE TUNERS into the tailpiece, insuring adequate clearance for ball end strings and checking that they operate smoothly. (A little beeswax is a great help.) Reinstall the endpin. Install the tailgut into the tailpiece, adjusting the knurled brass nuts so that, when under string tension, the lower end of the tailpiece is even with the lower edge of the saddle. Usually this will give about the right distance from the bridge to the tailpiece. Cut off excess tailgut length.

● Fit the feet of the BRIDGE precisely to the front of the violin and at the right "backtip" angle. See the diagram in "Useful Measurements," page 22, and "Violin Making, Step by Step," pages 66-70 for details of bridge fitting. (You really need this book, or a good teacher, if you're new at cutting bridges.) The bridge height is set with the G and E strings temporarily installed. The upper edge, its curvature, thickness, and grooves are then completed.

● Apply a little GRAPHITE lubricant from a No. 2 pencil to the nut and bridge string grooves.

● Now install the STRINGS in the "upward pegbox" order, G, E, D, A. The strings are wound so as to end just snugly at the side of the pegbox, not jammed against it. This enables smooth, secure tuning, without danger of the peg coming completely loose. High quality modern compound steel core strings give excellent sound, are more stable and durable than the gut or synthetics, and are a better match to the convenience of fine tuners.

● Select and install a suitable CHINREST. Many teachers do not recommend the flat "Guarneri" style for young students, however usual among performers. An *edu* or low *Teka* gives better security and comfort. Avoid the waffle-grid types. For those few students whose chin straddles the tailpiece, a "Flesch model without the hump" is recommended. SHOULDER REST selection is best left to the player or teacher, but don't stock any that damage the instrument.

● Play it and adjust the bridge position and angle, post, etc. and don't put it on the shelf until it's right!

≥≈

Young Person's Guide to String Instrument Care

For More information, visit:
www.HenryStrobel.com
Copyright © 1999 Henry Strobel

Fitting the Violin or Viola - Hold it under the chin in playing position. If the left-hand fingers can comfortably curl around the scroll, with the elbow slightly bent, the instrument is not too large. Straining to play one too big can be bad for your music or your health.

Fitting the Cello - Sit with knees bent square, the C-peg behind the left ear, the middle finger of the left hand able to touch the top of the bridge. (The violin shop can replace a too short end pin.)

Fitting the Bass - Stand behind the bass in playing position, the nut level with the temple, the middle finger of the left hand able to touch the top of the bridge without bending forward. (Note - the normal "adult" size bass is 3/4, not 4/4.)

Chin Rests and Shoulder Rests - These should let you play comfortably and securely. Our local schools typically recommend a low, lightweight "Teka" style chin rest and an original "Kun" shoulder rest. Look out for worn pads that might scratch your instrument.

Cleaning - Use a dry untreated cloth to clean the instrument after use - a man's handkerchief is good. If you need to clean or polish it, use only a white liquid violin shop type. Have any cracks or openings repaired first, wipe it on with a clean soft paper towel (not the dry cloth kept in your case!) and rub it all off. Keep it away from the strings, bridge, peg holes - and bow!

Bow - Don't polish the bow, or touch its hair, or wave it around. Don't drop or drag it on the floor, or touch anything but the strings with it. Tighten it just enough to play right, and loosen it after playing. Remove the bow before taking a cello or bass out of a soft case, and replace it after putting the instrument back. Round rosin is best. Rotate it as you apply it - it will last longer and not become grooved. Take your bow to the violin shop if it loses hair or becomes warped or "slippery" or cannot be adjusted.

Strings & Tuning - Use the right size strings. They should be wound just to the side of the pegbox. Tune the pegs slightly lower, then slowly up to pitch, no higher, pressing in slightly. If pegs slip or stick, have them checked by your teacher or corrected at the violin shop. After a while tuning pulls the bridge toward the fingerboard, which can make it warp or fall or affect the tone. The tailpiece side of the bridge must be kept vertical. Ask your teacher to show you how. Use fine tuners with steel core strings, but preferably not with gut and synthetic strings. If the tuner screws go in too far unscrew them (but not enough to buzz) and retune the pegs. Sometimes a sticking tuner screw can be fixed by removing it and rubbing it on a wax candle. If not, have the violin shop replace it.

Problems - If the fingerboard, sound post, or bridge comes loose or breaks, or if you find cracks or openings, loosen the strings right away and take it to the violin shop. If the strings buzz or dig deeply into the bridge, or feel too high or too low take it to the violin shop. Never glue anything yourself - and don't let your Dad - and certainly not the bridge or sound post!

Protecting Your Instrument - Don't leave it in extremes of temperature or humidity. Don't leave a cello or bass standing at a wall. Place it gently on its side on the floor, but only when you can't put it in its case, which is the safest place (it doesn't abrade the edges and protects against classmates falling over it). Use a "suspension" case if possible, flat on the floor. Close it securely before picking it up. If you must use a soft case, get a thickly padded one and beware doorways. And don't leave an instrument or bow in an open case on the floor - or on a chair for the careless or absent-minded to sit on or knock off.

Henry Strobel & Sons Violin Shop Repair Job Log

Name	Telephone	Repair Description	Date In	Date Done	Date Out

COMMON REPAIR PROCEDURES

If you are (or have on your staff) a qualified professional violin maker you can undertake work on more expensive instruments or more complex work, such as restoration or grafting. Basically, we are only talking about less expensive instruments and simpler repairs in this book. You have to know when to say "Sure," "No," or "I don't know." The information here is in addition to that already provided in the other books, and is not complete in itself. There is nothing exotic here, just things we do over and over in day to day work on ordinary instruments. You will become very familiar with the contents of *Useful Measurements for Violin Makers*. This is basic stuff, but often overlooked by busy repairmen.

String Replacement - Strings are replaced as needed, not in sets. Steel strings on elementary violins may literally last for years. On the other hand, the fragile aluminum winding on some cello A strings seems to disintegrate immediately at the nut. You may wait a bit if the frayed part is in the pegbox, not in the playing part. Contrary to what many teachers think, this does not mean the (steel) string is about to break. Its strength is in the steel core. But if the winding is worn or stretched and strings do not play in true fifths of course they must be replaced. The integrated fine tuner tailpieces are preferred to separate ones especially on the tiny fiddles. Synthetic or gut strings are not well suited in either fit or function to fine tuners. Their tuning range is limited for these "stretchier" strings; they tend to cut the softer strings and add weight. Gut strings are short lived, unstable, and expensive, but the performer or advanced student will have his own good reasons for using them. See *Useful Measurements for Violin Makers*, page 19-22, for basic string information. A sample form is shown on page 21, which can be adapted to monitor minimum string stock in the small repair shop.

Bow Maintenance - Time was when all school bows were indestructible, easy to rehair fiberglass. Now very nice wood bows from China are sold (in my shop, at least) for as little as $25, much less than rehairing at $40-50. These disposable bows are a win-win proposition. The student gets a fresh clean bow with his rental, and the shop does not have to rehair them. (Sorry if you are one who thrives on rehairing bows in bulk - there is money to be made if you are good and fast, doing several an hour.) Save your energy and precision for rehairing the good bows - and please don't tie the hair with wire! You will find that some of these bows are a bit warped and have to be straightened over your kitchen cooktop. A bit of the "good" warp (to the left) is OK. Or they may have too little or too much spring. In the past the problem was weak sticks. Many of this new breed of bows are quite stiff and may have to be "desprung" a bit to avoid tip breakage problems. See that everyone has a good cake of *round* rosin.

While the recent availability of good and very inexpensive wood bows has occasioned a sea change in our approach to student bows, another change is on the horizon with the advent of inexpensive carbon fiber bows. These will perhaps soon provide the student with permanent bows of good and stable characteristics, but we will have to go back to rehairing them until they reach the "disposable" level. On the other hand there are now new very inexpensive upgraded "fiberglass" bows available from the original and other sources that offer to rehair these in bulk at $10 each.

Rehairing and the other common bow repairs are treated quite thoroughly in *Violin Maker's Notebook*, pages 7-26. The method there is a good one, but if you have learned to place the hair in the head first or install it dry, these can also be good methods. (These books do not cover the authentication and restoration of very expensive classic bows any more than they do of such instruments. Such expertise has to be learned on the job in specialist shops.) The invaluable technique of splining broken bow heads was shown in *Violin Maker's Notebook*, page 20. It can also be used for broken German bass frogs as here:

Buzzing - is a rattling sound from arco or pizzicato. It is not a wolf. Finding its cause may be more difficult than fixing it. The rate and timbre (metallic or woody) may be a clue. Here are some of the common buzzes -

Strings buzzing against the fingerboard. Obviously the bridge or nut may be too low, but it is not always so simple. Very often it's because the fingerboard is warped, uneven, or lacks the required longitudinal concavity. Sighting along the fingerboard gives you a rough idea, but you need to place a steel rule on the board and look from the side with a light opposite. You may find that the rule actually rocks over the high spots, which may be general or localized. Learning to plane fingerboards rapidly and right will be a most valuable skill. Of course planing is typically a correction for old worn fingerboards with the pits and furrows of use, but by far the most common need is on new inexpensive student instruments where it was never done, or where the wood has shifted, shrunk, or warped after assembly, or after delivery to the student. This sadly may cause him to think the playing problems are his fault. The use of unseasoned wood, especially by new factories under time and price pressures is all too common. Use care in stacking or shipping cellos to not place pressure against the boards, which can warp them down, or, with the bridge down for shipping, tighten strings against the board. So many unnecessary problems could be avoided. Another marginal cause of buzzes are the position marking tapes placed across the fingerboard on elementary instruments. Some of these have a significant thickness and may require more clearance.

(Other examples of **problems from unseasoned wood** are pegs that are out of round or drift too far into the pegbox, shrinkage cracks in the lower front, endpins where the ebony or "rosewood" has shrunk away from the hole and/or tightly onto the shaft, and fingerboards which have shrunk leaving sharp edges along the sides of the neck. But I digress.)

A truly sharp, well adjusted plane makes the difference between a pleasant and a nearly impossible job. Use about a six inch plane for violins, violas, and about a 12 inch for cello and bass. Normally it is best to leave the fingerboard on the neck, but to remove the nut for clearance. Practice to master the art of

long fast sweeping strokes with enough momentum to not stop or dig in, landing on the board just above the lower end and lifting off near or at the nut end. With eye, feel and straightedge, you will learn to do it perfectly - or well enough. Always specify ebony fingerboards on instruments you procure. Hard epoxy "ebonizing" paint will quickly dull your lovely plane and leave unsightly white areas difficult to stain and finish. After planing, block sand with medium dry, then fine wet sandpaper. Immediately give a brisk rub with a paper towel, which will leave a matte luster, showing up any remaining defects. No need for oil or French polish.

Openings (loose glue joints) buzz when the mating surfaces slap against each other. The most common buzz is when the front or back becomes unglued from the rib. Check for this by "thumping" around the edges with fingertip or knuckle. When located, run in a thin palette knife to clean the opening and to glue, lightly on the front, more strongly on the back. (Gluing, clamping and cleanup are covered in the other books.) Less frequent, but more troublesome, are woody buzzes from loose linings or blocks. They are hard to definitely diagnose, and involve the decision to open the instrument to get at them, and the faith to be sure you've got them all before closing the instrument. Probe with a palette knife and tidily glue anything loose. It is easy to suspect a loose bass bar, but this is almost never the case except, rarely, where the instrument has been in a serious accident.

f-hole wing tips can buzz loudly if they are clogged with varnish and touch. Make sure they don't touch.

Buzzes at the Nut
1. Buzzing **against the fingerboard** near the nut (arco or left hand pizzicato): If the nut is too low it has to be raised. (If the fingerboard has to be planed do this first.) Raise the nut by removing it and fitting a thin layer of wood ("veneer") under it, dyed black. Or, make a new nut of ebony if the instrument merits it. As always, refer to the tables in *Useful Measurements for Violin Makers* for adjustment data.

2. Or the string **buzzes in the groove**: The string must leave the nut at its bottom edge, where it joins the fingerboard. Of course this means that the strings will all be stopped at the same length, but

perhaps more important, it prevents the string from buzzing in the groove of the nut. Be sure to check this by pressing your finger on the string if there is a buzz. It is really amazing how loud a buzz a bass string can cause this way.

Tuners or any loose metallic parts can cause a high-pitched buzz. Test by touching suspicious bass machines, fine tuners, chinrest hardware (or chinrest touching the tailpiece). The cello endpin is a frequent source of buzzing, either at its mounting plug or at it's innermost end, where the small pin or cotter key that retains it in the cello may rattle. In this case a bit of thick glue applied to it with end of a dowel will do.

Neck Repairs

Broken at the body end, or at the scroll end, or resetting neck angle. See *Art & Method of the Violin Maker*, pages 68-70. Another unusual break is in the middle of the neck. I described an elegant way of repairing this without a graft in *Violin Maker's Notebook*, pages 71-73. (I should also point out that where the break is longer, or on an inexpensive violin with a thick fingerboard, you might possibly simply reglue it since the much of the strength of the neck is in the fingerboard.)

Gluing

Gluing is an art for the violin maker. It is described throughout the books, but I would like to mention here the glue I have found to be best for high quality professional work. See Milligan & Higgins under Some Special Sources. Actually, glue from any violin supply house is probably OK. *But please remember – use no white or yellow glue or "liquid hide glue" on bowed string instruments!*

Securing the Saddle

Some cellos and basses have the saddle set only halfway through the front edge, a bad idea as the saddle tends to tilt up under the pull of the strings. Cleaning out the old glue and regluing with strong hide glue will probably last, but you may want to install a conventional full depth saddle.

Crack and Damage Repairs

This is a major, wide subject, and cannot be fully treated here. Please refer to *Violin Maker's Notebook*, pages 27-39 and 67-73. Note too the back soundpost patch "workaround" (the Brits would say "dodge") mentioned on page 16. Really, it's more important for the purpose of this book to say what one should *not* do rather that what to do.

Be conservative; you or someone else should be able to undo or redo what you did. This means not removing any original wood or varnish as far as practical. Never ream out peg holes unnecessarily; always reduce the oversize peg to fit. Never sand to level cracks that did not quite line up when glued. It requires a difficult long retouch procedure and is never quite right. Never sand worn or frayed edges; removing more material is no solution. If there is no time to restore the missing edges simply seal them with several coats of clear spirit varnish. But clean them first; never varnish or French polish over dirt, please.

Cleats on cracks are often unnecessary. Use of a wire to pull a cleat in is especially deprecated. A new method of clamping inaccessible cleats uses the new extremely strong rare earth magnets. I have not used this method yet, but it's another example of learning new techniques through the violin makers' online forum I described on page 20. The suggestion is to go to www.stewmac.com and search for "magnet."

Cleaning and polishing

See *Violin Maker's Notebook*, pages 36-37, for a **more complete discussion.** Denatured alcohol is good for removing rosin and dirt from bows, strings, fingerboards bridges, and chinrests. To keep from spilling alcohol on the varnish remove the small parts for cleaning. For the fingerboard or strings, which stay on the instrument, use a paper towel dampened with alcohol. Don't make the mistake of using the "scotchbrite" abrasive pads with alcohol-they will drip profusely when compressed. If you do spill alcohol on the varnish, let it dry. If instead you wipe it off you may wipe the varnish off with it!

For cleaning a rosin crust off the front of ordinary school instruments, a diatomaceous earth rubbing

compound, e.g. Meguiar's No. 4, is good, but should not be used on fragile or fine varnish. (It's also great for rubbing down new varnish!) Use a 6mm thick felt pad, McMaster-Carr no. 8834K32.
Note: Before using alcohol or Meguiar's for cleaning, consider trying Simple Green, page 15.

After cleaning, generally the white creme **polish** is used on the **instrument**, wiping it on with a paper towel and continuing until it is wiped off, leaving only the shine. (*Hammerl "Joha"* polish 8740e/8741e is the standard example.)

French polishing, which builds up a microscopic layer of spirit varnish on the instrument is not necessarily desirable, occluding the natural texture of the varnish, but it is a good way to seal worn areas, as where the hand wears away the varnish from the upper right rib. It is also usually a good finish for the bow stick and the neck.

Peg Repairs

See *Violin Making Step by Step*, pages 62-64 for **fitting replacement pegs**. The cardinal rule here is to shave the peg rather than ream the hole as much as possible to conserve original wood - and not to end up with big holes!
Redrilling the string hole. As pegs wear they migrate into the pegbox, sometimes placing the string hole at the far side of the box, preventing its tightening. You may be able to simply drill a new string hole near the center of the box. Of course it is your choice whether to trim off the excess peg extension - or simply replace the peg, which may not fit very well anyway.

Refitting the peg. Another reason for pegs not holding is the existence of a slight "shoulder" on the peg just outside the box. Sometimes the taper in this region can be corrected, improving the fit without requiring a new peg. The peg will however move farther into the pegbox; see the previous paragraph. In any case the peg must fit well at both ends and be liberally treated with Hill's peg compound.

Bushing Peg Holes. Bushings are installed when the peg holes are too large or not quite in the right place, or an adjacent crack needs reinforcing. (For this last an internal or external inlaid "cheek" may also be

used.) The traditional bushing is a tapered fine-grain hardwood dowel, such as boxwood. (A spiral bushing gives good reinforcing and is less obtrusive visually, but probably not warranted on the ordinary instruments we are discussing here.) Use care to remove no varnish in trimming the glued-in bushing flush with a razor sharp chisel. Otherwise the instrument is degraded and careful retouching is required.

An alternative to the tapered boxwood bushings is paper based **phenolic cylindrical tubes**. These are strong, "wood-colored," don't split, and can be shaped, reamed, glued, and varnished well, but are hard and hard on tools. Find grade Xx Garolite Hollow Rods tubes of suitable inside and outside diameters in the McMaster-Carr catalog (see their address on page 17).

Bridge Fitting

Clearly one of the most frequent and critical tasks for any violin shop. Critical indeed for the professional musician but extremely frequent for the student shop. Practically every new student violin will need a new bridge fitted, or at least refitted. I cannot begin to describe this here, but you will find detailed information in *Violin Making Step by Step* pages 66-70, and in Cello Making Step by Step pages 58-60.

Study and refer to the comprehensive **adjustment tables and bridge templates** in *Useful Measurements for Violin Makers*, and especially to pages 21-22 for the overall **standard diagrams for violin and cello**.

Fitting bridges fast and right is an indispensable skill. You will absolutely need to have a set of templates, a sanding jig for fitting the feet, and to become adept at using the bench sander (without losing your fingertips) to thickness the front face. Naturally you will finish every bridge with file and knife, but you cannot afford a lot of time to get to that point.

Installing Bass Bridge Adjusters

This procedure was not described in my other books, so is presented in more detail here. Like cellos, string clearance on basses varies with the season

(humidity). To adjust bridge height for this, as well as playing styles you may be asked to install these. This was not covered in my other books, so here's an illustrated procedure, using National Coarse threads.. (In this bridge the short sloping legs dictate the wheel placement.) Drill the upper legs with an appropriate smaller size for tap, no. 7 or 13/64 in.

Saw out 1/4 in or more from the legs, leaving the feet just high enough to keep the adjusters clear of the instrument front. (Some temporarily, using paper between, glue the back of the bridge to a piece of wood to facilitate cutting on a table saw.)

Some treat the upper leg holes with cyanoacrylate for a stronger, more homogeneous thread material. Thread with NC coarse 1/4x 20 tap. Drill holes in the feet for a free fit a little over 1/4 in or about 6.35 to 6.5 mm. Smooth the sawn edges, taking care not to change the angle.

Apply beeswax to the threads and lower shafts of the

adjusters. Finish the top of the bridge for the correct shape, string action, and adj. range.
Ream these holes from the bottom *only* for "play" to independently adjust for height. (Not shown.)

The Sound Post

I presume anyone reading this will already know how to set a post, and it is mentioned in several contexts in the books, but be sure to refer to page 23 in *Useful Measurements for Violin Makers*. The cut card shown there for measuring the post position is perhaps my most frequently used tool.
Remember this rule: *A good starting distance for the*

post from the bridge (lengthwise, edge to edge) is equal to the thickness of the front plate at the post.

LABOR CHARGES AND RATES
". . . for the labourer is worthy of his hire." Luke 10:7

Truly, we cannot simply characterize the work of violin repair as *labor*. It is not like a pieceworker digging fence post holes. Each job may turn out to be different, with different problems to be solved. Some of the tasks are quite technically demanding, requiring something like the skill and responsibility of, say, dental work. Further, the skill of different repairmen will vary, and correspondingly the speed and worth of their work. So it quickly becomes clear that *actual* hourly rates are unusable unless they are based on standard skill levels and times. The most fair and practical approach is to charge by *nominal* (flat-rate) fees, for example $15 to fit a new bridge on a fourth grader's fiddle, but $60 on a professional violin, regardless of how long it actually takes. It has to be done right, and you may expect to work longer while you are still gaining experience, but be able to complete the job later with expertise. In other words you are paid for what you know, not for simply what you do.

Repair pricing is one of the more interesting (even vital) questions for anyone in business - or it should be. Not so simple either. Analogies range from the auto mechanic to the country doctor.

For some, repair is the main business, and attracting the work and maximizing return is the goal. For others, repair is a necessary evil, done primarily to satisfy and keep customers and keep them from going elsewhere, or because it's the right thing to do. (I'm in the second category.)

Flat rates - this is more or less the norm. There are some assumptions. The job must be definable or quantifiable - as tuning a piano, making a bridge, or bushing a peg, although there are variations in difficulty, and time, in every particular job. Another assumption is that you do the job right, in a competent, workmanlike (yes,"professional") way. These flat rates are somehow related to average hourly labor costs, and to what the competition is charging, but only secondarily to the actual time spent. Far better for the customer to have the work done perfectly and quickly than to have it done poorly and slowly. (But gouging or harming the customer is reprehensible as well as bad business.) Flat rates simplify and average things and give the customer a standard expectation. For example, in

rehairing bows, some will be more difficult (glued-in plugs), some easier (reusable plugs), and some will use less expensive (black) hair. Based on average experience one can adjust the flat rate.

While flat rates are the norm, they are not invariable. Like the good country doctor, many of us will modify the actual charge, lowering it for the good student or mom who can't pay more, or for good teachers, or as a sales tool. Rates may rise for the more difficult or demanding repair (or customer). Skilled luthier labor is in short supply, and most shops prefer to use it on their own inventory (either to restore it or of course to create it), rather than rent it out by the hour

A friend of mine suggested that he preferred to keep his repair prices fixed except when he wanted to do someone a favor or as a charitable donation, in which cases he charged nothing. He felt that lowering the price was telling the customer that he was charging arbitrarily and could take less, and that it degraded the status of his work. At first glance this sounded dubious, but upon reflection it is something that we probably all do to a degree, at least where relatively small jobs are concerned. We may not want to "nickel and dime" good customers who make sizable purchases from time to time by charging for small adjustments.

Having said all that, the question of exactly what these flat rates should be remains. They can vary with your location, overhead, clientele, and reputation. If you belong to a trade association you may be influenced by its internal rate surveys or recommendations. Or you could ferret out other shops' rates and adjust them for your own situation. My rates happen to be lower by comparison, but I am not going to say what yours should be, nor could I. Comparing rates between shops without a standard of comparison is unrealistic.

But yes, the craftsman is worthy of his hire. The conscientious, competent repairman should hardly earn less than the auto mechanic.

Note: we are talking about customer repairs as such, independent of sales, guarantees, etc. You may be doing a lot of maintenance work on your fleet of rental instruments, for example, and you will have make sure that these costs are adequately covered by the rental program profits. You will need to do these jobs fast and efficiently. More on rental programs later in the **Sales Chapter**.

ﺍﻟﻠ

Please note: All dollar amounts mentioned below are simply relative estimates, variable with time and place.

Small Shop ("Real-World") Rates

In general, jobs are priced by material (list price), and actual labor (for example, nominally $50 per hour). The time for a particular job will be more for painstaking work on expensive, professional Items, less on school equipment.

Some representative or average labor prices are given on the next page. With appropriate adjustments, these can serve as guides for charges in a typical shop, where frequent interruptions make the accurate recording of time spent difficult.

These prices on the next page are for labor only, except for bulk supplies such as hair, silver wire, glue, varnish, small wood pieces, etc., which are not individually accounted for and are included in the job charge. Thus the price for basic rehairing of a bass bow reflects the larger amount of hair used compared to a violin bow, etc.

Some jobs are nearly all labor, for example, crack repair, and vary with the complexity and degree of concealment required. Most major jobs will not have sample rates but are charged for the actual time required. Resetting a neck, for example will vary widely in difficulty and time from case to case. Removing a top or back will vary widely in difficulty depending on the strength of the glue and condition of the wood.

Other minor jobs are nearly all material, for example, new strings. I charge list price if installation is provided, or give a discount for a sale only.

Individual parts, such as ivory tips, bow screws, pegs, and bridge blanks are not included in the job price and are charged separately according to the kind and quality of the part used.

Replacing the bar, or fitting a sound post patch, for example, always requires the separate additional charge for removing the top. Likewise reinforcing a separated button, for example, requires the separate additional charge for removing the back. Resetting a neck for correct projection may require a new bridge.

Terms: cash or credit card on delivery, of course.

Based on time:
Use the nominal hourly labor rate and give a conditional estimate before accepting the work. Examples of such work are repairing cracks, removing front or back, varnish repair, neck resetting, front or back inlaid post patch, rebar*, reinforce broken button, major cleaning and rosin removal, etc. Such jobs are too variable to charge as standard jobs. But don't short-change yourself on the estimate (the final price can go *down* too), although unforeseen additional difficulties often appear once you get into the job.

Based on standard job charges ("flat rate"):
Mark up a table like the one below to fit your particular situation. You can fill in your prices and add as much detail or as many variations as you find convenient. Note that
- All are subject to change for unusual circumstances. - Jobs marked with * are plus material.
- Prices are in US dollars.
- All jobs include any required retouching.
- Some jobs require others. For example, the charge for removing the front is added to the charge for replacing the bass bar.
- V=violin or viola, C=cello, B=bass

Bows	V	C	B
Rehair	40	45	50

(includes ordinary cleaning, plug(s), wedge, if needed, good white hair, black for bass)

Camber	10	15	20
Straighten	15	15	25
Spline head	60	60	80
Shorten hair	10	10	15
Rewedge	10	10	15
Polish	10	10	10
New eyelet	10	10	20
New pearl slide	30	30	35
Bone tip	60	70	80
Plastic tip	20	20	30
Silver wrap	50	60	60
"Shrink" tubing wrap	7	7	10
"Whalebone"	30	30	35
Leather Grip	15	15	20
"Shrink" tubing grip	5	5	7

Note: good rental grade new wood bows can now be sold for:

	30	35	40

Fittings	V	C	B
Fit new student bridge*	25	45	65
Fit new professional bridge*	50	80	125
Rework bridge	10	15	30
Fit new post*	15	20	30
Reset fallen post	7	10	15
Plane FB	30	40	60
Refit peg	5	10	
Fit new peg*	10	15	
Bushings (pair)	30	50	
Adjust nut	10	10	15
Fit new nut	25	35	45
Fit new saddle	30	40	50
Fit new "tailgut"	10	15	25

Install strings (no charge if bought from you at list, otherwise charge 25% of lis, but strings, especially European, have such high list prices, and are so widely discounted, you may have to be flexible.)

૨૪

The **small shop charges** data above may be all you need to adapt for your "real world" repair or rental shop. But for further information and perspective I have given below a more detailed schedule of typical? rates for upscale shops. These will seem high by comparison, and indeed the majority of the student instruments we encounter could not be repaired at all at these rates. *I am not suggesting that you use them.* They are illustrative of the repairs and rates for expensive instruments in highly professional, high

profile, high overhead shops. They tend to be arbitrarily set, and will vary from one third to triple those shown! But remember that these repairs have to be near perfect and unobtrusive, which may require extra time for coffee, planning, retouching, and perhaps redoing. *Liability when working on hugely expensive instruments is also an important factor. Some of these repairs (actually "restorations") require specialists, and few small shops can or should undertake them.* I have not included the myriad exotic bow repairs here. Only the professional bow maker (not I) will be doing these, and I trust he will know what to charge.

Some of the repairs done in restoration shops are questionable or inadvisable, and it can be argued that they should not be done in either the "real world" or the "fancy" violin shop. Such include **regraduation, back doubling, full edging, and revarnishing.** Their outcome may be unpredictable and they can be very expensive, but they are grist for the restorer's mill. They can change, for better or worse, the original character of the instrument, but there is often an overriding profit motive in correcting the mistakes of the original maker (or subsequent repairmen), turning a functionally poor instrument (even a wreck) with an attractive or plausibly attributed name into an auction miracle. I guess we could call this "value added" restoration.

૨૪

"Upscale" Shop Rates

(We can't fairly categorize shops by small and large. Some small shops are very professional and expensive. Some large shops have low prices by economy of scale.)

Bridge	V	C	B
New student bridge	50	90	135
New prof. Bridge	80	150	250
Bass adjuster wheels			100
Rework bridge	20	30	35
Parchment (each)	5	10	15

Clean /Polish	V	C	B
Minor clean	10	25	30
Clean & polish	50	100	115

Pegs, Pegbox	V	C	B
New Pegs (set)	80	120	
Bushings (pair)	60	90	
Cheek (each)	150	200	250

Soundpost	V	C	B
Fit new	30	40	50
Adjust	15	20	25

Fingerboard	V	C	B
New fingerboard	220	400	600
Plane inc. adjust nut	50	75	110
Reglue	35	55	65
Shim or wedge	150	200	250
Raise projection	80	100	

Neck	V	C	B
Broken at heel/pegbox	135	175	250
Neck graft, inc. fb	1000	1500	2000
Reshape, retouch	175	250	275

Front	V	C	B
Remove & reinstall	175	275	375
New bass bar	350	500	600
Restore arching	500	900	1200
Breast patch	600	1000	1800
Breast cast	100	150	200
Full cast	250	400	600
Replace corner	80	90	100
Half-edging, ea. bout	200	300	400
Full-edging	700	1000	1500
Soundpost patch, cast	300	600	750
Regraduate	200	400	600

Back	V	C	B
Remove & reinstall	250	350	450
Button graft	500	600	700
Button reinforce	250	350	650
Button ring, ebony	130	160	200
Replace corner	90	110	130
Soundpost patch, cast	650	950	1200
Regraduate	300	500	700
Doubling	1000	1500	2500

Sides	V	C	B
New block (each)	150	200	350
Glue opening (each)	10	15	20
Reinforce rib (each)	100	150	200

Miscellaneous	V	C	B
Saddle, new	50	60	75
Nut, new	40	50	60
Install bass extension		300 to 600	
Tail"gut"	15	20	35

Cracks, including any cleats and retouching -
estimate time individually.

TECHNICAL UPDATE (The State of Violin Making)

(This piece has little to do with repair shop work, but I was looking for a place to write it down, and found one here. HS.)

The world of violin making has never suffered a lack of enthusiastic crackpots and rascals, and the tradition persists. But by far the great majority of us are decent, dedicated craftsmen working in a field we like, stepping around the land mines of artistic subjectivity, commercial greed, and sometimes suspect "science" to help enable our fellows with valuable, affordable musical equipment.

The violin developed out of art, in the broad sense, and was dependent on science, in the modern sense, neither for its birth nor significant improvement. Out of all the "papers" published, few have provided compelling advancements for the violin maker. In the aggregate, however, we have learned better ways of thinking about our art, and a better scientific understanding of how violins work, although much energy was spent by "follow the leader" makers who more or less superstitiously vibrated and scraped disassociated plates in the hope that this, hardly more than a quality control technique for components, would somehow result in great instruments when the parts were put together.

So what have we learned from science about violins? Perhaps not that much *practically* that good makers did not know before, but we know it more securely and by the correct names now. Out of my forty years or so of immersion in the "literature" of the violin and from my work with violins, here are some of the things that strike me. Sorry, no footnotes, merely my distilled impressions.

(This first is from history, not science.) Old violins are different from new ones. Not necessarily better. Early violins were made differently and for different music. Most have been modernized (changed and improved). Much of the credit for an old violin goes to the restorer and to "show business" rather than to the original maker.

Old violins are older! **The wood** has changed internally over time, probably primarily and permanently from natural changes and environmental influences, and perhaps only secondarily from use. If there is an "old violin sound" it is probably because the wood is now different. (They did not look or sound old when they were new.) There is no evidence that main line classical makers ponded or stewed their wood, although these processes can give beneficial results to tonewood similar to those from age. Old wood has increased opacity, decreased hemicellulose and its adsorbed water, changes to the lignin, and changes to its damping, perhaps decreased at lower frequencies, giving good response, and increased at higher frequencies, giving a pleasing tone.

The secret of Cremona is not in the varnish (and in reality it is nowhere). But **the varnish** is an important tone factor. To the extent that it penetrates and changes the wood, varnish is *usually* a detriment, adding undesirable damping and mass. Varnish changes over time, drying and/or hardening (longer for oil), wearing off, becoming brittle (probably good), being reflowed or added to by French polishing and such (probably not good). The best policy is to keep the varnish out of the wood and to apply no more than necessary.

The particular wood selected for violin making has a major effect on the quality of sound and efficiency of the violin. Usually the ratio of stiffness to density is considered a primary **figure of merit** for the spruce soundboard, but we can go a step farther and say that for a given ratio the less dense wood is preferable. I do not think this oversimplified "figure of merit" applies for the wood of the back and sides. Here both flexibility and lightness seem important. This is of course complicated by the radiation mechanisms of the instrument, but my experience has been to make wonderful instruments, easy playing, responsive, with a nice dark lower register from a maple tree with very deep flame (hence flexible), which had been left out in the weather a few years after logging, with some of the "aging" effects similar to those of ponding and perhaps fungus.

The effect of **the arching** model on tone has always been recognized, as in the trite comparison of Strad vs Stainer tone, but in more recent times its huge effect on tone formants has been better appreciated. It's not just graduation anymore!

Playing-in has generally been thought to be desirable to bring out the best in a new or not recently played instrument. Measuring the subtle changes and identifying the manifold mechanisms involved is complex and has not yet been well done, but the fact that energetic vibration does something and can at least be used to bring an instrument into a standard "played-in" state for evaluation can hardly be questioned. What does it do? It probably does not much permanently change the wood itself, which is thankfully quite durable. It probably relieves stresses from moisture and assembly, and at least temporarily mollifies the rigidity of glue, glue joints (even purfling?), ground, and varnish. (I published von Reumont's book on this, not a "scientific" book but a good and unique book.)

The factors above are among those I call **"aperiodic"** or untuned. They are attractive to the maker, since good wood, for example, is good for instruments large and small. Good varnish and varnishing technique and stress relief are good in general.

Other factors are among those I call resonant or **"tuned."** (Doubtless not a rigorous distinction.) These apply differently to different instruments, sizes, and modes. Some of these are

Free plate tuning. This is basically graduating to compensate for differing wood characteristics to achieve a specific free plate vibration pattern. Not of itself a reliable predictor of instrument quality.

Wolf tones. The mechanism is well understood, and practical cures are readily available. (We have even traced the E-string squeak to a torsional vibration.)

Modal analysis of the complete instrument. Unlike free plate tuning it relates to actual completed instrument characteristics. If a maker has the requisite equipment and skill, more or less faithful "tonal copies" can be made.

A0 B0 matching. Tuning a basic air and structural resonance to each other may result in an apparently "livelier" instrument. More than that I can't say. Tuning the tailpiece by mass and afterlength is a related approach. Such adjustments are subject to change from replacing or working on fittings.

Having said all this, the fact remains that a luthier with experience and intuition, although untutored in science, can eventually make an excellent violin.

Further to that, a factory with excellent **quality control** and feedback (and a consistent stock of seasoned wood) can mass replicate that excellent violin rather reliably. I buy violins in quantity from several sources, and find that some are consistently excellent. True, many factories have "no clue" and repeatedly lose the recipe, but I see everyday evidence that it can be done, better perhaps, and certainly less expensively than by the lone artist maker reinventing his wheel. This is good news for young musicians, the traditional mystique which we all love notwithstanding.

≈

To keep up to date with progress in the science of lutherie, the best record is the *CAS Journal*.
www.marymt.edu/~cas/journal/

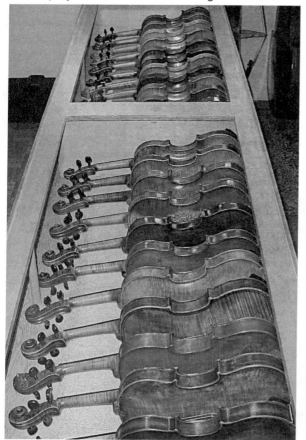

SALES

This trite quote is much over-used, but does have a certain poignant relevance to violin dealing. Before going on to the mechanics of selling things in your real world violin shop, here are some small tutorials to read:

Prices and Choices for Students
(From www.HenryStrobel.com)

Our policy - We are public service oriented. We do not play the "old violin game" of inflated antiques and dubious attributions, and we do not pay referral commissions, which covertly raise prices and bias the choice. We give large real discounts, and will not try to sell you something you don't need. We guarantee what we sell.

"Shoppers beware!" - Someone sees a brand or label on the internet, or in a music store, or in the paper, and calls to compare the price with ours. This is unrealistic. Is it the same model? What is its condition, its guarantee? Can you see and hear it before you buy, and be assured of expert, prompt local service? The most important thing is its adjustment or"setup" and its effect on tone and playability. A guaranteed professional setup with high quality strings, rests, optimal action, bridge, post and other adjustments costs us an additional $70-200. Are you getting this, or a fiddle full of obstacles for the student?

Well, what about brands? - When you buy a "brand x" new car, you know pretty well what you're getting, but violin brands and labels are often much less specific, not to say deceptive. They frequently indicate only the importer or distributor of that commodity. The actual source may be a variable "cottage industry" in an unspecified country (although better brands assure that the source is their own "workshop"). You may hear misleading slogans from dealers, like "You get what you pay for." (More likely you pay whatever they can get.) Another is "Instruments from _____ are inferior." This is a wrong and unreasonable generalization. For equal quality, instruments from a country with low labor rates should simply cost less than those from one with expensive labor. Excellent instruments are available from many countries, and in fact most high quality handmade student instruments are now made in China, and typically cost half as much as

comparable machine made instruments from most European countries. (Certainly we sell instruments and bows from European countries, US, Brazil, etc. as well, but a crude, unadjusted instrument is always a mistake, wherever it's from - and we don't have any of those!)

What about fine old and professional quality instruments? - People often say that sound is everything in choosing an instrument, but in fact they are influenced by many other things, easy playing, condition, appearance, price, and rightly so - they are choosing a long term personal partner in work and inspiration. Please understand first that there is no necessary correlation between the appraised value and the musical value, nor will an old violin necessarily sound better. (The fact that you or your teacher may like a violin says little about its actual worth or origin.) Anyone can get an adequate instrument without paying the "big name bucks." But many violinists will want something special or unique. This is part of the mystique of the violin. Besides the sound, they may prefer a genuine old instrument for its age and individuality. For professional performers, the "show business" factor comes in, often dictating an impressive sounding Italian or French "pedigree" to print in the programs. It is unfortunate that some young artists, pressed by teachers, conductors, or dealers feel obligated to acquire instruments they can ill afford and perhaps really do not need, and which often fail as investments, especially after the commissions are paid. Consider a less famous, or even anonymous maker. (We just might have the right "real world" artist bow or instrument for you.)
Note: Never take a label in an instrument at face value (especially Grandpa's "Stradivarius"). Take it to an expert.

Who's a violin maker? - Often first-time customers, having seen my sign, Henry Strobel, Violin Maker, come in, look around, and ask, "Did you make all these?" Well, certainly not at those prices! Some violin makers do only that, making expensive artist instruments, as I do occasionally, but those that operate violin shops may not have the time, being occupied with adjustment, repairs, customer service (and in my unusual case writing and publishing books for other violin makers). A violin maker is one who has proven expertise in making and working on violins. Whenever you need help with your instrument or bow, take it to a professional violin maker, such as you will find in a full service violin shop. Few music store technicians or amateur makers have the necessary specialized skills or tools.

Here's another:

What's in a Name?

It's not the old *"Stradivari"* from the attic or the new one from the local music store that I'm talking about. Everyone, except apparently their naive owners or the parents of beginning string students, knows about those. They have been supplied forever to impress just those customers. A larger question for readers of this book is that of instruments from violin shops, dealers, and auctions, where even the owner or seller may be unaware of the origin or evolution of his instrument.

One common practice is shop production of "artist" violins from imported white ones with or without dents, scratches, and "antiquing" added, graduation and bar changes (perhaps), varnish and label applied by the "maker." This pretty much allows the value-added "re-maker"/reseller to choose how to sell it - as made in the original country of origin or in his shop, or by the original white violin maker or by him. So, for example, a violin sold as made in Germany may have been regraduated, varnished and set up in the US. Not necessarily illegal or even wrong, but doubtless misleading (as marketing ploys often are). This has been going on for centuries.

It also happens that white violins originally manufactured in lower labor cost Asian countries, are imported to Europe, varnished and sold as made there, perhaps with a house brand label (usually the name of a dead or imaginary maker, in effect a "brand" of the importer or exporter). This takes advantage of the unfounded but still prevalent perception that European instruments are somehow essentially or generally preferable to Asian ones. The legend "handmade in ____," was and is frequently added, serving to indicate that the largely machine-made or foreign-made instrument was at least

finished by a hand-held spray gun! Partial truths seem to be traditionally and openly acceptable in the violin trade, even if out and out fraud is (usually) not. A rumored example is a new violin ostensibly made in the storied city of Cremona, Italy, which was in fact a good quality Chinese instrument varnished, set up, and sold there. One should critically ask whether, in any case, an instrument carved in Cremona is *ipso facto* preferable to one carved in say, Oregon or Bulgaria or Beijing. There is a lot of overpriced pseudo-tradition being sold. A variation on the realtor's mantra "location, location, location."

We should note too that many expensive, collectible violins, even if they are better functionally than originally made, are hardly the same because of the extensive modernizing, repairs, restorations, regraduation, new varnish, new wood, and (not least), new label. "What's in a name?"

I have never been a dealer in expensive antique instruments. This is a problematic practice suited only to those with the appropriate expertise, orientation, and guts (which I frankly lack). Those I have sold in my violin shop have been sold on their own evident merits or based on my cost. *Wishful thinking* does indeed affect the violin market and those dealing in it. The larger dealers of course in most cases maintain the practice and perception of ethical dealing, given the tenuous bases for authentication and the hyperbolic prices related to rarity and perceived artistry more than to functional excellence or material and workmanship. But in the area of "attribution" some are on shaky ground indeed. Here is a small, true anecdote. A minor dealer showed me a violin that he was puzzling over to determine how he should sell it. I indicated my opinion that it was a mediocre specimen not likely to be identifiable as that of a particular maker. Sometime later the violin was shown me by someone who was considering buying it. I was indeed surprised to find that it had been fitted with an "Italian" label apparently deemed plausible by its seller. This would not be so bad if the new label actually stated that, as an attribution or ascription, but in fact it had been artfully covered with a thick layer of dust that could not possibly have accumulated by natural means in the intervening time! Determining authenticity or assigning authorship is a minefield for the expert, folly (if not fraud) for the ordinary fiddle dealer. See the *Connoisseur* chapter in my *Violin Maker's Notebook*. And the article on Roger Hargrave in the June 1992 *Strad* contains quotes worth repeating:

"At the moment we have a sort of *Glasnost* in violin making and makers are learning to tell each other the truth. Who knows, perhaps they will soon start telling the customers the truth as well."
And:

"I am sure that Chanot and Vuillaume didn't make fakes - they made copies. But then the real difference between a copy and a fake is not how it is made but how it is sold."

Later, in the October, 2000 Strad, he notes:

"One of the great weaknesses of connoisseurs is their tendency to become infatuated with lofty ideas and ideals. In spite of the magnificence of Cremonese instruments, violin making was (and still is) a traditional, repetitive craft, where technical proficiency came before artistic inspiration. However, almost since the time of the violin enthusiast and dealer Count Cozio de Salabue (1755-1840), connoisseurs have largely ignored this fact, preferring to perceive violin making as an art form. As a result, individual makers were elevated to the status of artists, a process which altered the perception of Cremonese instrument production. Inevitably, the myth of the lone individual making one-off masterpieces became firmly established, although the reality was somewhat different."

This revelation, not new, but rarely stated, already appears to have already had an effect. - I received an auction brochure listing ". . .important Italian violin made under the direction of Antonio Stradivari, Cremona, c 1707"

In other words, the nominal artist maker may not be the actual physical producer of the instrument and of its parts, but perhaps only its designer and production supervisor and quality controller. This occurred in the master as well as the mediocre shops of the past, and in even more blatant modern practice. For example, a proposal was made to supply me with instruments made to my own model, drawings, and specifications and of my own wood and varnish by highly skilled personnel using advanced tools and techniques. Although these instruments might possibly be better than my own, and multiply "my" production, I was, needless to say, not interested. But once again: ". . . the real

difference between a copy and a fake is not how it is made but how it is sold."

Let me hasten to say that the artist makers of my acquaintance are above reproach in this area. They take far too much pride in their art to do otherwise. However in the case of "shop made" instruments there may be, particularly with the passage of time, difficulty in distinguishing these from those made individually by the master of the shop.

For *authentic new instruments* sold directly by the maker, the value is the price he sets, and whoever buys one buys it on its own perceived merits. *Caveat emptor*, and be sure the instrument is as represented, i.e. as made by him in all its parts, and not, God forbid, a white violin he has finished, which would be something altogether different, and worth a small fraction of an artist instrument's price.

For *presumably authentic (one can rarely be sure) old* instruments the market value consists of two components: One is based on the original, authentic maker, rarity, artistic merit, and condition. The other is "value added," from the improvements by restorers, the provenance of famous owners, performers, and the large prices paid in the past. If an instrument has been considered to be excellent, authentic, and valuable, it is likely to continue so and more so, this being more significant to buyers than the technical accuracy of attribution.

In other words, the value of an instrument is what buyers will pay for it, never mind that this value is inflated by factors of provenance (who played it before), "show business," conductors' recommendations, teachers' commissions, expected appreciation, and the perceptions of the "market." While the musical excellence of these renowned instruments is often touted, it is often subjective, variable with time, humidity, and adjustment, and one can nearly always find a far less expensive or anonymous instrument that is equal or superior in performance.

Unfortunately these perceptions tend to pressure musicians into spending a disproportionate amount of their income on the tools of their trade, their *instruments*. While any artist might understandably want an artistic instrument made by an individual luthier, as opposed to a mass produced one (however functional), entirely suitable, affordable instruments are available from modern or lesser known earlier makers.

While the authentication of the actual maker, place, and time is more important fiscally to the collector and investor than functionally to the performer, it is interesting to ponder the countless examples of mistaken, fraudulent, or unsubstantiated attributions. We see such a narrow range of names for sale considering the number of instruments and the plausible number of makers. In a trade where merchandise is habitually made to resemble someone else's and is so labeled, and where there are large numbers of items looking very similar, it is largely on faith (good, we hope) that many items are traded. This is particularly true of bows.

Violin dealing has traditionally been a trade fraught with questionable practices, but nowadays it can be very big business, and this business is frequently a blatant example of conflict of interest, where the appraiser and seller (or buyer or agent) is likely to be the same person, or are at least closely associated as colleagues, perhaps in collusion. Some transactions are byzantine, involving additional parties and percentages and practices quite unknown to the nominal seller and buyer.

Seller and Buyer

These two comprise an unstable system, like a two-legged stool or a teeter-totter. It is only in balance or equitable when the dealer is both expert and honest and the buyer (or student) is knowledgeable and knows what he wants. Otherwise the sale can tip to the advantage of the dealer or simply go nowhere, as often happens when the student is unable to make up his mind, and his parents declare they know nothing (perhaps true), nor naturally do they feel comfortable taking the dealer's advice. They are looking for help, and this often comes from:

The Teacher

Add the teacher, and the equilibrium of the three-legged stool can be realized. A choice can be made, and a good choice, insofar as the teacher, like the dealer, is both expert and trustworthy. But what sometimes results is more of a "Bermuda triangle."

The teacher, as respected master and mentor, has

great influence over his student's choices. Surely, he or she deserves compensation for any extraordinary consulting services in helping the student make the best choice, but an openly agreed fee, not a percentage, paid to the teacher by the student, is the best solution. What are these services worth? Time and travel expenses, certainly, and expert advice (although the expertise of many teachers' in instruments amounts to little more than "what they like"). Alarms go off when I hear that a teacher has told a student that he is at the point where he should be looking for, say, an "x" thousand dollar violin, as though there were a direct proportion between market price and musical value. There is not - but there may indeed be between market price and a commission secretly paid the teacher by the dealer. This is potentially big business for both - the teacher gets paid and the shop gets an easy sale. Over time the teacher may come to regard this as his due, and the shop as a cost of easily doing business.

It may be more likely for the private teacher, who seeks to upgrade his student's violin, to enter into this "networking" with dealers. The dedicated school classroom teacher, whose school and many of whose students are impoverished deserves our help and respect, and by and large will be selflessly appreciative of our efforts to provide their students with decent, affordable equipment. More on this in the next chapter.

If a dealer is not a "team player" he may never hear from certain teachers, or may notice that their students take his violins out to try but never buy them. He may resent the teacher's casting aspersions on his wares and services, although such suspicions must usually be suffered in silence. Further, even if his instrument is attractively priced by comparison it may be rejected, since "You get what you pay for." (How wrong that often is!)

Of course a teacher is justified in shunning a dealer whose wares and services really are inferior. And he has a right to work with and favor those whom he likes and respects. Likewise, the ethical dealer is quite right to appreciate and help good teachers. While he states and observes his strict policy of not paying teacher commissions, he may from time to time do small favors for teachers as long as they are unrelated to any particular sale or to a percentage of sales. This is common sense, although it might appear improper, unless they are *small*. Typical such reasonable favors are free rehairs of the teacher's personal bow, or referring students to such good teachers. This latter is in fact not really a favor at all, but is simply right, just as it is simply right for a teacher to recommend good dealers, or good instruments.

We aren't talking about this here - only about the abuse of hidden commissions, which can harm
- the student who unknowingly pays an unspecified fee to a salesperson he knows only as his objective and impartial advisor, and
- the dealer who does not pay such commissions and may thereby be excluded from sales and his products perhaps belittled in the process.

For many teachers and dealers this practice is something simply "inherited" and the teacher might understandably take umbrage at criticism. I have said more than I really intended to about this, but it does confront anyone in the business. For example, the respected dealer Charles Beare of J. & A. Beare, London, told the Violin Society of America Convention in 1988:

" . . . the payment of commissions to members of the teaching profession. . . has been going on since time immemorial. My father tells me that in the depression we paid up to 20 percent on lesser instruments and still had a turnover of under £300 a month at times. Our firm gave up paying commissions over fifteen years ago and I cannot say that business has declined, although there were a few teachers whom we never saw again. Many times I have urged dealers to work against the practice, but I have come to the conclusion that it will eventually be the associations of the teachers themselves who will outlaw it, although perhaps not just yet. Many teachers, of course, genuinely have the best interests of their pupils at heart, and are unswayed by considerations of commerce in watching over the search for the right instruments, but it is certainly true that others make a nice little sideline out of it. I have never met a dealer who thought that the practice as such had anything in its favor, but I have spoken with many who have told me that business is steered very firmly away unless the customary percentage is offered. This is why I feel that any initiative aimed at eliminating the custom should come from bodies representing the teaching profession, and I would urge them to think about it."

Congratulations are due *Strings Magazine* for speaking openly in recent years on this usually "unmentionable" hot potato. For example see *An*

Elegy for Ethics? by Susan M. Barbieri, *Strings Magazine*, May/June 2002:
www.stringsmagazine.com/issues/strings102/ethics.html

Strings has also been good about pointing up the excellence and practicality of modern instruments for professional performers. Much of the old and rare violin mystery, worship, and the related coffee table book phenomena amounts to sales promotion as much as to "art and archeology." Fine arts sales, like contests and advertising are bound to be subjective and of course highly competitive; the big thing is not to be naive about it.

String musicians and teachers tend to be conservative in taste, and are also frequently led by prejudices learnt from their teachers or from dealers. They may disproportionately prefer the old, and particular old names, frequently leading the student to pay more than he can afford while receiving less musical value. Customers will often say, as they should, that it's the sound, the way it plays, that matter, not who made it, etc. But they will quickly drop their favorable impression of an instrument they are trying upon being told that it is German or Chinese. A fiddle with a mellifluous name, true or false, from Paris or Cremona will have an edge, and if that's what the buyer wants that's what he'll get. We often see a particularly benighted bias when it comes to non-European made instruments. This may be partly related to the interest of dealers and owners in maintaining and increasing the prices of their old or restored instruments.

We read sensational news stories of fabulous sums paid for old violins. We also read occasionally of fraud in the trade in such instruments. This is nothing new. Fiddle faking, forging, and fraud has been going on for hundreds of years. I have a copy of the Strad Magazine, No.6 of 1890, its first year of publication. You may find this article from it by the author of the classic *Violin Making as It was and Is* interesting.

"*Old Violin Frauds*, by Edward Heron Allen.
. . . a subject of constantly recurring interest. I refer to the unscrupulous and daring frauds, that are continually being practised upon the public, by certain dealers in violins whose code of morality appears to fall far short of that which regulates the actions of the most hardened dealers in horses or old masters. Year after year at the Old Masters' Exhibition the council of the Academy open the

Catalog of Professional Books for Violin Makers

and for Anyone Working with or Interested in Bowed Instruments

Henry Strobel, Violin Maker & Publisher
10878 Mill Creek Road
Aumsville OR 97325 USA

Send Email to: **Books@HenryStrobel.com**

For more information visit us at: **www.HenryStrobel.com**

IOLIN MAKERS Fourth
c handbook. A standard
and comprehensive. For
bass and bows, all sizes.
ent. Tables and text.
ons. Bridge templates.
grams. Illustrated, with
. . . . $12.50

hird (Expanded) edition
. Rehairing & repairing
retouching instrument
safety. Instrument
al intervals. Illustrated.
lines, and annotated
connoisseur . . . 19.50

, AND CELLO
on the Acquisition,
nent, and Conservation of
by Lucien Greilsamer.
nry Strobel from the
. . . . $9.50

YS (Fine hardcover)
raphical, philosophical.
ies, illustrated . $19.50

P Henry Strobel has
for over twenty years.
nd technical details of
outfits, forms, customer
o make a decent living
to students, musicians,
. . . . $29.50

TEP BY STEP" (Violin
Making a cello as an
obel demonstrates and
ures used by the violin
se-up and complete, it
s. Three NTSC or PAL
ins. $99.50

BY OTHER AUTHORS:

NCE CONDITIONS OF
RATION-DEDAMPING.
iolin maker. By Prof. G.
. . . . $29.50

STRUMENTS OF THE
nce and Art) by Jan
ng" for string musicians
. . . . $22.50
)

REVIEWS —

(The series) "All are thoroughly illustrated . . . replete with bibliographies, annotations, and indices.

The *Art & Method of the Violin Maker* is . . . a very personal account, written with great erudition and insight. . . . "All these titles are recommended to anyone with even a passing interest in violin literature."

(Cello Making, Step by Step) ". . . contains a wealth of valuable information . . . Strobel's motivation . . . is purely and simply to help someone out here share in the great pleasure of building an instrument to be proud of. I am sure he has already succeeded many times over."

From reviews by John Dilworth in *The Strad*

(Useful Measurements for Violin Makers) "I hardly know another book where a maker can find all the important measurements in such a clear order. . ."

Karl Roy, Geigenbaumeister, Mittenwald

"It is such a pleasure to read something sensible about the violin and its world. . . . It is also refreshing to read literate English on this subject. . . "

Norman C. Pickering, Past President, VSA

(My Real-World Violin Shop) "This is probably the only such book in existence and Henry has achieved his purpose very well. Nicely written . . . a very welcome bargain."

Leonard Showalter, Editor, SCAVM Bulletin

"If you have your own shop, or plan to set one up - even if you only plan to do a little repair work . . . or sell one or two of your violins - then you NEED this book."

David Brownell, Editor, MVA *Journal*

(Health of the Violin, Viola, and Cello) ". . . a great wit and humor about it . . . Strobel's translation is wonderful . . . In addition to his other talents as engineer, luthier, scholar, and author, I believe there must also be something of the poet."

Robert Lundberg, Luthier, in *American Lutherie*

(Violin Making, Step by Step) ". . . is clear, systematic, and full of good information and advice."

("Watch Me Make a Cello, Step by Step"-VIDEO) This is organized to be useful to the first-time cello maker. Strobel shows both traditional hand tool methods (and) power tools . . . With ideas also for the advanced or professional maker, this video displays ways to plan and organize to do "good honest work."

David Brownell, Editor, MVA *Journal*

(Violin Making, Step by Step) If a beginner could own only one book . . . I'd have to recommend this one above all the others.

Sam R. Compton Jr, Member, Board of Directors, VSA

(Setup and Repair of the Double Bass) "So I am happy for the bassists in New York, and now the whole world, that Chuck has been able in this book to share his insights . . . with his characteristic humor; knowledge (based on experience), and concern that each bass sound as beautiful as possible."

Ron Carter, NY

SETUP AND REPAIR OF THE DOUBLE BASS FOR
OPTIMUM SOUND First Edition 2005. By Chuck Traeger
with David Brownell and William Merchant. Well
illustrated, 377 pages, 8.5 x 11 in. This big book is the bible
for the bass, complete on repair and sound optimization. A
lot of it applies to other instruments too. There's never
been a book like this . . . . . . only $85.00 plus shipping*.

BOOKS ORDERED:

ITEM —	Each	X Quantity =	$ Amount
Setup and Repair of the Double Bass . . .	$85.00	ISBN 1-892210-06-1	$_____
Violin Making, Step by Step	$29.50	ISBN 0-9620673-6-9	$_____
Geigenbau Schritt für Schritt	$29.50	ISBN 1-892210-04-5	$_____
Viola Making, Step by Step	$25.00	ISBN 0-9620673-9-3	$_____
Cello Making, Step by Step	$29.50	ISBN 0-9620673-7-7	$_____
Art & Method of the Violin Maker	$19.50	ISBN 0-9620673-5-0	$_____
Useful Measurements for Violin Makers	$12.50	ISBN 0-9620673-2-6	$_____
Violin Maker's Notebook	$19.50	ISBN 0-9620673-3-4	$_____
Health of the Violin, Viola, and	$9.50	ISBN 0-9620673-4-2	$_____
Reflections (Personal Essays)	$19.50	ISBN 1-892210-01-0	$_____
My Real-World Violin Shop	$29.50	ISBN 1-892210-03-7	$_____
"Watch Me Make a Cello, Step..." NTSC Video	$99.50	ISBN 0-9620673-8-5	$_____
"Watch Me Make a Cello, Step..." PAL Video	$99.50	ISBN 1-892210-00-2	$_____
How to Improve the Resonance Conditions. . .	$29.50	ISBN 1-892210-02-9	$_____
Practical Acoustics of Instruments of the Violin Family	$22.50	ISBN 1-892210-05-3	$_____

AIRMAIL **inside** US or Canada for **each** book
or video $4.00   _____ $_____
*(Exception: $9.00 for the *Setup and Repair of the Double Bass*)

AIRMAIL **outside** US or Canada for **each** book
or video $5.00   _____ $_____
*(Exception: $18.00 for *Setup and Repair of the Double Bass*)

TOTAL AMOUNT: $_____

BILL AND DELIVER

NAME ( )   _____
   or
COMPANY( )   _____

STREET   _____

CITY   _____

STATE or PROVINCE ___

ZIP or POSTAL CODE ___

COUNTRY   ____

E-MAIL ADDRESS ____

SELECT

( ) MAIL ORDER WITH C

MAIL this order form with pa
videos, and postage by CH
on a US bank to:

Henry Strobel, Violi
10878 Mill Creek R
97325 USA

- - - - - - - - - - -

( ) CREDIT CARD

Card No. __ __ __ __ - __

Expires __ __ / __ __ Name

Signature _____

MAIL this credit card order

Henry Strobel, Violi
10878 Mill Creek R
97325 USA

or
FAX it to Henry Strobel:

- - - - - - - - - - - - - - - - - -O
Or, simply and securely, O

www.H

eyes of picture fanciers to the frequently doubtful correggiosity of their cherished Correggios, and year after year the musical public is startled by the exposure of violin-swindles, the perpetrators of which defend themselves with an assurance that is positively cynical, citing in their defence " the custom of the trade," and that much abused legal maxim; *caveat emptor.*

"A long experience of violins and violin-dealers, combined with a close acquaintance with the leading violin-collectors and connoisseurs of Europe and America, has put me in possession of the facts connected with some of the most daring frauds that have been practised on the gullible amateur, by dealers whose names are, or ought to be, considered as guarantees of the good faith of their transactions, and in the last decennium these cases have been of such frequent occurrence, and have been so imperfectly understood by the public, that a brief review of their salient points may be considered by your readers to be neither untimely nor uninstructive. . .

"The *cause celebre* of Hodges versus Chanot which shook the violin trade to it's foundation in the year 1882, is within the memory of most of us, and certainly in its published result no case ever produced such a false impression upon the minds of the outside public. The facts were, shortly, these. In August 1881, Hodges called upon Chanot and expressed his desire to purchase a "speculative violin," and was shown a violin which he declared to have been represented to him as the work of Carlo Bergonzi, the most celebrated pupil of Antonius Stradivarius, of Cremona. Chanot called his attention to the doubtful character of the instrument, and gave practical proof thereof by accepting for the instrument the sum of £55, about one third of the then recognised value of an authenticated Bergonzi. No warranty was asked for or given, but Chanot undertook to support Hodges with his opinion, should the authenticity of the instrument be called into question. *Hodges, however, made it a condition of the purchase that Chanot should give him a receipt for £20 more than he actually received, a practice unfortunately much in vogue among professionals who purchase instruments for their pupils, and gloss over this form of deliberate theft by the use of the euphemism "commission."* (emphasis mine) Hodges then negotiated for the sale of the violin to the well-known collector Mr. J. L. Cooke, at the price of £150. Mr. Cooke, on seeing the violin, expressed his doubts and insisted that it should be shown to William Ebsworth Hill for his opinion. That opinion being unfavourable, Hodges returned the violin to Chanot, the matter culminated in the Queens Bench Division on the 11th of February, 1882, and during the trial some statements were made which horrified the public, though the cognoscenti were well aware that the practices openly confessed to by the defendant were matters of everyday occurrence. Hill gave it as his opinion that the violin was the work of a then almost unknown maker, named

Johannes Franciscus Pressenda, a pupil of Storioni who worked in Turin at the beginning of the century, and then Georges Chanot was put in the box where his humorous and cynical nonchalance in exposing the secrets of his trade made, for him, a most unfortunate impression upon the court and upon the jurors. He stated that he had bought the violin in Paris and had himself inserted the label " Carlo Bergonzi, Cremona, fecit anno 1742," which label he had taken from an old mandolin by that maker, and went on to say what is well-known to all fiddle-fanciers, that it is the custom of the trade to put into violins, labels of the makers who possibly or probably made the instruments. I possess, as curiosities, sheets of these labels, printed in old style, on old paper by a Parisian firm, for the use of the trade. Sir William Field, now Lord Ventris, before whom the case was tried, remarked very justly that there is no harm in making copies of old instruments so long as they are not palmed off as originals. At Mittenwald and Mirecourt there are factories that turn out hundreds of instruments every day, modeled on those of the old masters, and labelled with their names, but no one is deceived by any one of them . . ."

True, no one, I hope, in the trade is deceived by these, but nearly every day regular folk earnestly confide to me that there is a paper inside Grandpa's "very old" fiddle that says "Stradivarius." On being enlightened, their incredulous response is "Well, why would they put that in there if it weren't true?"

On a somewhat loftier level of wishful thinking we read the names of makers in the lists of auction results. It is not to hard to conclude that some of these makers must have been supernaturally busy to produce that many items. In fact a great many of them were either produced as fakes or by employees or were made by decent unsung artists but have been renamed to the "golden canon" of makers for profit. The auction records should show many more makers' names than they do. However, as time goes on and the source of plausible fiddles shrinks, the canon of great makers is augmented as lesser makers are discovered and promoted. Truly a *golden* canon. The provenance of Pressenda would not now be painted-out! Years ago I repaired one for a collector (read private dealer), who had bought it for about $4,000 quite some years earlier. The front had later been revarnished (not by me). I think it sold at auction for approaching $200,000.

SOURCES OF INSTRUMENTS ETC.

In the past I did a little selling and consigning of old instruments but have not for many years. Here I am speaking mainly of new or used instruments for the beginning (rental) or advanced (upgrade) students such as are appropriate for a small real world violin shop. These are standard, functional items that have more or less established prices. This book is not a guide for the antique dealer.

What's it worth? If you don't know, you shouldn't be selling it. If it's something you personally made, you are quite free to set the price, and it will sell or not based on your own skill and artistic appeal. (It has gratified me to note that instruments I have made myself will normally sell for tenfold what a functionally equivalent "no name" will sell for.) But most of what we will be selling in the "real world" violin shop will be commodities, affordable factory or "shop" instruments. You will develop a set of sources for these. These suppliers may sell merchandise with or without a house brand (or a real brand in the case of distributors), and with or without a list or "manufacturer suggested retail price." Resellers like yourself, and like music stores, can set or manipulate your "list" prices. We do not, although it may be adjusted to include special setups, strings, or accessories included.

If the supplier does not assign a **list price**, there is more room for you to "buy low" and sell high, if that is your focus. (Our personal aim has been to provide the best value to more students.) The most common markup in suppliers' catalogs from the dealer's net price to the suggested retail price is 100%. Our (highly unusual for a full service violin shop) advertised policy for practically forever is that we sell at list less 25%, thus essentially splitting our profit with the customer. This has worked for us - we feel pleasantly generous and have lots of happy customers. (Our accountant is not particularly pleased.) Most small shops will prefer to charge list or more based on their professional service, but we do have to be realistic in this discount-oriented world, when our customers can buy strings, etc. from catalogs or the internet at close to our own cost. Even with our reputation we have to emphasize price, and especially service.

Try to get suppliers who are responsive and on the near side of the country. This saves customer waiting time and shipping costs. Even for ordinary repair parts and small supplies like strings, rosin and shoulder rests, it's good to develop at least one reliable supplier who will get things out the same day

you call. No need to comparison shop and "nickel and dime" here; it's not worth it. Treat your suppliers right and they will treat you right.

Inventory - where to get stuff. Suppliers of bowed instrument merchandise vary, and the quality and price of their products certainly do. I need to be circumspect here and can only speak in general terms about categories of suppliers. I do have personal experience of many suppliers. The safest and most reliable are of course those with established good reputations who have been successfully in business for many years. They will have gone through the initial learning curve and are more likely to be using established quality control procedures and seasoned wood. Even these suppliers may have occasional lapses, but will cheerfully correct them.

Another kind of supplier has a wider range of instruments (including plucked, brass, etc.) with the lowest prices. They are typically less particular about who they sell to. (Perhaps this is why they require payment in advance or COD.) Their house brands are typically those one sees at small resellers on the internet. They are more likely to buy "commodities" from the low bidder in emerging countries. The quality may thus be spotty, and they may have less expertise in strings. On the other hand, some of their lines are likely to be very good value indeed, particularly for rental equipment - avoid the bottom lines like the plague. But you must be ready to do or redo the "factory adjustments" and plane the fingerboards (ebony only please). Be also ready to explain to your customers why the instrument they saw on the internet is not comparable to the one they are getting from you.

Unfortunately for us in the real-world violin shop there are an increasing number of suppliers who will sell to anyone. They have both wholesale and retail catalogs, differing little in price. We don't need to reward this kind of undercutting by buying from them - there are a plenty suppliers of the "regular kind." There are undeniable attractions to the musician, moonlighting teacher, online customer or avid Ebay bidder to this direct buying. But they may overlook the services and expertise that we provide. This is really what we have to offer.

The "regular" traditional wholesale violin supply houses generally require assurance that you are a legal bonafide reseller, such as a tax identification number or state sales tax number. (Oregon still has no state sales tax!) Once you are an established customer, you can normally buy on open account, which gives you some flexibility in paying. Also it's easier to return unsatisfactory or excess merchandise if you haven't paid for it yet. Even though they may have an internet presence, you should find a statement there something like this.

"Welcome to our website. Please note that we are a wholesale company, and do not sell directly to the public. We will only accept orders from retail dealers and luthiers. If you are a musician, teacher, student, or other end-use consumer, and would like to review our quality line of stringed instruments and accessories, please click the "Locate Dealers" button above!"

The Chinese are coming! No, the Chinese are here. It is simply a fact that, for equal quality, instruments from China can be much less expensive because of lower production costs, and may also have a higher proportion of fine hand work because of lower labor costs and less mechanization. This is highly competitive, and the trend seems to be ever lower prices with increasing quality. There is no shortage of importers of instruments from China, and some of the better ones may in fact come to you in a truck driven by a salesman. You can pick out some beautiful stuff this way. (This same method is common in the fine bow trade, where, once you are established, representatives of the artist bow makers in Brasil will visit several time s year for you to select bows.) Mass hand making of inexpensive instruments has always been the province of specialist areas with strong craft traditions and low labor costs. As some of these (European) areas become industrialized, their violins may appear more "factory" like, and as other emerging countries learn the craft they begin to provide exceptional value. See page 49 for **Classes of Student Instruments**.

Time was when a preferred upgrade instrument for a student was an older European one, even a "brown German." Some of these are indeed very nice, but the majority are better suited to make lamps or

shadow boxes of when compared with the better new instruments.

Practically all the instruments we carry (except my own) are below $6,000, and the majority are under $1,000. Beyond that you are getting into major complications of consignment, appraisal, certification, trade-ins, and all manner of competing dealers, teachers, and violinist colleagues getting their oars into the water. Beyond that level there is relatively little correspondence between musical and market value, and the value hinges on names, associations, and authenticity, and you had better have the stomach and expertise to back it up. I am not well adapted for that, and I am not the first person to look at an old instrument, irregularly sculpted of plain wood, without quietly wondering whether performers who pay such princely sums for such professional tools must be some notes shy of a real-world scale.

Now we need a few words about **appraisals**. Appraisals and certificates of origin/authenticity are different things, but the former depends on the latter. That is, you cannot say what something is worth unless you know what it is.

Be careful here. There has to be a good reason to stick your neck out. You should not be appraising things unless you have a lot of experience selling them, and of course you should not be selling things that you do not know. So the first rule (obviously) is to limit appraisals to the class of equipment that you *know*.

Most appraisals are for these reasons -
- to state (or update) the replacement value of a customer's equipment for his insurance.
- to set the fair market value for a consignment sale in your shop
- to suggest what to ask for in a private sale

Appraising should not be viewed as a profit center. It is more trouble than it is worth. Charge a flat or stepped fee, not a percentage of appraised value. It should go without saying that your appraisal will be objective and unbiased by any conflict of interest.

If the item is obviously an ordinary "attic Strad" it's best to advise the customer that it's really not worth appraising. For routine appraisals charge a small flat fee for a verbal, a larger flat fee for a written appraisal. This should be on your letterhead and clearly linked to the equipment appraised. The best way to do this is to include verbatim the contents of any label(s) and to include a photograph showing distinctive wood grain, the appraiser's equivalent of a fingerprint. The photo can be taken almost instantly with a simple digital camera, printed onto the back of the appraisal and signed. The usual verbal description of the instrument is quite lame - hardly necessary to note that it is made of maple and spruce, or that the back is in two pieces. (If the back were in one piece of black walnut, that would be worth noting!) The traditional recording of over the arching measurements can point out unusual sizes, but is practically useless for identification. See the example on page 59. This is about as far as I care to go, and only for a favored customer. (Yes, these look far better in color when printed on my Deskjet.)

Suggested typical **written appraisal fees** (may vary with difficulty and complexity) for:

Valuable items you sell	Free
Instruments you did not sell	$50
Bow	$30
Insurance claim letter	$40

Verbal appraisal fees (your choice)	Free to $30

Certificates of origin are best avoided altogether. If the equipment is of the readily recognized type there's no need for one. If it's not it's usually very hard to be sure. Don't play the flaky attribution game, the mother of conflict of interest. All is not forgiven by "In my opinion . . ." any more than by *caveat emptor*. One case in which a certificate is highly recommended is when selling your own work. Who can guarantee and describe it better than you?

Read *The Connoisseur* on pages beginning on page 58 of my *Violin Maker's Notebook*.

Consignments are the essence of "dealing." You are the commissioned broker for goods you do not own, like a realtor. Related to this is accepting goods from suppliers to be paid later, sometimes called a "floor plan." Either way the idea is to be in a position to make a profit without prior expenditure and risk. I

have little experience of this, and personally prefer not to be a hired salesman for anyone. (We own everything in our shop, but that is practical only because we are selling modestly priced merchandise.) Consignment sales are in fact the normal *modus operandi* of regular violin shops, if not of our real-world kind. Generally it goes like this. The owner agrees to place the item in your shop for sale at an agreed upon price for a specified period, to pay you up front for any reconditioning needed to make it salable, and to pay you a percentage of the sale price, typically 20 to 30. There are variations on this - some dealers (big ones too) will simply agree to pay the consigner an agreed sum upon sale and will retain anything over that. Caveat consigner!

ந

In the competitive and fuzzy world of the violin it is important for you to have standard published policies and adhere to them except when you are feeling more generous - never the opposite. Always give customers something they weren't expecting. It might be as little as extra time and courtesy, setting up a fallen post for free, or a good cake of rosin, or a free case with a violin purchase. This makes a powerful impression, even a bond, as it ought. It builds good will and is remembered and passed on to others and marks you as a generous person, which indeed you are.

ந

Never criticize your competition, even though they well may criticize you, especially if you are the new man moving into their territory. Competition and the bottom line is a powerful driver, and once you cut into others' sales, or appear likely to, other businesses may unscrupulously malign your reputation. You have to prove yourself and be above this. Emphasize the differences and the better service and prices you have.

And advertise! Word of mouth free advertising is the best kind, but does not happen overnight. After taking care of any tax or permit matters for your new business the first thing to do is place an advertisement in the telephone book yellow pages. This is expensive, but at least a minimal ad establishes your presence for anyone looking. (Even my small box ad shown full size on page 54 costs $1700 per year.) Less expensive and very effective are the ads you place in the concert programs of local orchestras, school and youth symphonies. These and contributions to their silent auctions, etc. benefit both you and the music programs.

The Public School Connection

If your area is fortunate enough to still have healthy string programs, there are several areas that may be attractive to the real world violin shop, but that may have little attraction (insufficient profit) for the upscale shops. These are **repairs** and **supplies,** and **bids to supply** new equipment. The schools have to use a competitive bid process, so it isn't easy or lucrative, but may work for a low overhead operation. Schools will as a rule, and understandably, expect a larger discount than you give your regular customers. Over the years we have done a fair amount of school repairs, not because we have solicited it, but because we do it reasonably, promptly, and right. Each year the school purchasing department usually issues us blanket purchase orders for a limited amount of repairs and supplies.

We have also bid on various local sealed bid purchases over the years, and were the successful bidder more often than not. This requires a certain tolerance for bureaucracy, and the margins are low. Naturally you need to have developed good relations with suppliers to competitively bid such jobs. As a local bidder you may receive a slight preference for being in the state and providing additional local services, but you are at a disadvantage in bidding against out of state companies, essentially agents who will drop ship to the school. Being local you will be expected to unpack, inspect, and setup the equipment. While the school will be less likely to trouble out of state suppliers, you will be asked to take care of any problems on the spot. Adjustment of string instruments is everything, and you must be prepared to assure this. Even so we have found such business worthwhile sometimes, considering the overall contacts and public relations aspects. For example we recently supplied $60,000 of string instruments for the opening of a new high school. An upscale violin shop might easily make more profit on the sale of a single classic instrument, but we had the satisfaction of public service as well as the showcasing of our products to a lot of teachers and students.

Rental or Rent to Own

This is a service needed everywhere that there are students. In some cases private string teachers provide rentals for their students, but usually it is the province of the music stores and violin shops. It is one of your potentially most profitable areas, and it both enables young students to get started without a major expenditure or risk, and at the same time grows future customers for you. Your rental "fleet" grows as you add new instruments, and as used ones are returned to the pool to be re-rented. All the instruments are well maintained, and no distinction is normally made between new and used at the elementary level. Being a violin maker you have an edge in having the maintenance and repair skills in house, which the music store may have to contract out for. Here in the Salem, Oregon area, our shop starts about two hundred and fifty string students each September, mostly public school fourth graders. Of course others, younger and older, start (and stop) during the rest of the year.

There are countless contract variations in different areas and shops, but most fall into the simple rental or rent to own categories. In the latter, payments, or a portion of them, apply to ownership or trade up. See the sample rent to own contract on page 55. We have tried to keep this simple and complete on a single page. It's the form we usually use. Where it works best is for the first and second instrument. At any time, the current instrument can be traded in and whatever was paid on that instrument is applied to the next. In cases where the child is starting with a tiny instrument and going through multiple sizes with different durations this method may not seem to work quite right, and we will make adjustments if appropriate. It is important to remind the parent that
he is really paying for usage and maintenance and trade up credit over a long time - it doesn't *all* go to ownership of the final instrument, except where that is the second instrument.

Many variations are possible, and you should choose another or modify this sample plan for your local requirements. You can also offer an optional rental only contract, which may be a better fit for small children who will be growing through, say, 1/16, 1/8, 1/4, 1/2, 3/4, and 4/4. The rates will be lower, and there are no complications of ownership, old or new, and trade in credit. The actual usage is simply paid monthly, two months minimum in advance (like a security deposit). Such a contract form (page 56) can be used when anyone needs to rent an instrument for a short period. You will as a matter of prudence want to limit such rentals to used or less valuable equipment to avoid instant depreciation or excessive risk of loss, or you may want to require a substantial refundable security deposit.

To further compare the advantages and disadvantages of rent vs. rent-to-own:

Rent-to-own provides a continuous upgrade of your inventory ("rolling stock"), as students drop out or sell the instrument they have paid for or pass it on to a younger sibling or - we hope not - trade it in elsewhere, or lose it in the closet. It also encourages a kind of commitment to musical education, considering the investment.

Rent-to-own is attractive to the student especially on a 3/4 instrument, since he is actually paying down on the quasi-final full size he will trade it in for. It may also be attractive to the beginner with a small violin since rent paid is simply gone, but an owned violin can be passed to another parent or child. The trade-in credit is only for what was paid on the current instrument being traded in - it is not cumulative. The difficulty is with the intermediate sizes. If a parent keeps trading in frequently - we had a child who went through three sizes in nine months! - he may well feel he is not getting his money's worth. The trade-in credit of the second instrument typically may be very small. In such cases we will provide an additional equitable discount on the new one or simply exchange for a larger instrument as we would in a simple rental. (A Solomonic decision, so to speak, not, we hope, not a battlefield one. The last thing you want to do is quote the letter of the contract to a harried mother.) Or the customer might simply keep the old violin and buy another at cash discount or open a new rent-to-own contract.

Simple rent is potentially the most profitable to the dealer, and there is no trade-in to complicate the cash flow. He happily collects rent for many years on the same equipment, repairing and upgrading it of course as appropriate. Title to the instrument is clearly his, since the customer owns no part of it. I'm not sure of the legal distinction here, but have never

had occasion to find out.

We also offer a simple **"starter cash discount sale."** It is about 45% off the rent-to-own total contract price, against which it credits at trade-in. The buyer has to decide how likely the child is to continue, as a purchase requires a larger initial outlay.

Our violin shop business is strictly local. You might even want to do this over the internet, but that is a whole different thing. For me it's the personal aspect of the business that has me doing it at all.

We have to talk here about the matter of credit and loss. Credit is the essence of a rental program. There will be some defaults, which have to be factored in, but you have to take this in stride. There aren't as many permanent defaults as you might think - parents and musicians' parents especially are nice people and most will pay if they can. Rationalize absorbing occasional small losses as public service. We may be the exception, but we have never turned anyone away, even lacking the "required" credit card, nor have we ever turned an account over to a collection agency, and we still have a successful business. Who wants to take away a kid's fiddle? Naturally we try not to put out valuable instruments to apparent poor credit risks. This attitude, that "the customer is not the enemy," has gained us priceless good will with the schools and community.

Having said that, there is one thing that can help tremendously with collection, and that is asking for a credit card. (It may end up being a grandparent's card -and that's probably the best kind.) Recommend that they let you bill it "automatically," but if they opt to pay by check and don't you can charge the card. Installing our credit card terminal made life so much easier. (For simple purchases checks are preferable since the 3% credit card fee is avoided.)

The downside of rent to own is the huge amount of bookkeeping required, sending statements when needed, and when someone brings in a violin years later to trade up to the next size you have to promptly pull up his payment record in the computer showing the credit to apply to the new instrument, etc. I am fortunate in being married to a congenial and efficient accountant who has everything organized in *QuickBooks*. If you do not have a "Susan" of your own, you may want to think twice before going into this side of the business.

Classes of Student Violins
By Size and Age

Pre-school

In the 1/32 to 1/8 sizes, these present special challenges in tone and setup. Basically two levels, a "can't bust em" thick-built cheap one that sounds like a bumblebee, and a lightweight, thinly graduated one that sounds more or less like a violin and costs several times as much. Parents who want "the best" for their child, and some private teachers will be quite particular about these instruments. Because of their size they are difficult to work on in the areas of strings, pegs, soundpost, fine tuners and shoulder rests. Comfort yourself that these will be relatively infrequently required, although if the child (or parents) persist you will be going through many stages.

Basic sturdy **beginner's** outfit with plain maple, ebony fingerboard, metal tuner-tailpiece, wood bow, plus good rosin, better steel strings, shoulder rest, adjusted. Cost in 2003 about $115 plus your adjustment. Rent to own at $15/month times 24.

Elementary Starters and Intermediates

In this and all the classes avoid anything without an ebony fingerboard. This usually marks the difference between a substandard and a real violin, but there may be acceptable exceptions. For example, as ebony becomes more expensive alternative hardwoods, whether black stained or not will become acceptable if the instrument is otherwise OK. Buying better quality for rentals will pay off later, although the payback will not be as immediate. Better sound, less setup labor, and the better appearance of flamed maple will be more attractive and justify higher rates

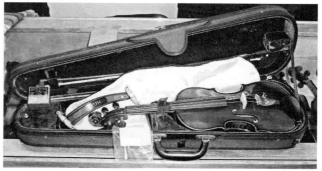

High quality **intermediate** well graduated, flamed maple outfit with good steel strings, fine tuners, plywood case, good wood bow, rosin, shoulder rest, wiping cloth. Comparatively lightweight and great sounding. 2003 cost about $225. Rent to own at $25/month.

than the shiny orange heavily sprayed lacquer ones of plain wood (some of which you will need in order not to exclude many beginning students).
Steel strings with four fine tuners are nearly universal here. In a few cases these may come with usable strings, but usually we have to replace (at least) the upper two with better damped steel strings to get a sound more like a violin than a banjo.

We usually have three grades; plain wood, handsome wood, and beautiful wood and sound. Currently for violin/viola these correspond to rent-to-own rates of $15, $20, and $25per month, whether new or used. These are **outfits**, including case with back pack straps, good wood bow, Hidersine round rosin, Kun shoulder rest, and polishing cloth. Rates are *approximately* double for cello, triple for bass.

High school/college level (except for the "uppity"). Certain brands have consistently superb sound and top workmanship. Handsomely flamed one-piece back. 2003 cost about $450, list about $950. We sell (cash discount) at $712.50.

We can now (2003) get wonderful cellos like this grand sounding and beautiful *Montagnana* model from China. Fortunate students buy instruments like this for well under $2,000 in our "real world" violin shop.

Obviously these rates would not be possible with expensive European instruments. Even so the rent-to-own price over 24 payments is well over the list price. This category spans 1/4 to 4/4, and while we like to keep the quality of full size instruments higher in general than that of fractional ones, there is a cost consideration for the fourth grader who needs a full size instrument. Here we have to provide an inexpensive instrument and hope that he will upgrade later and not embarrass us by playing it the rest of his life!

Note: *Violas smaller than a 4/4 violin are usually actually violins strung and tuned as violas, which simplifies the inventory significantly, since they can be converted back and forth as needed. True 14 " violas are common and optional.*

High School or College

Here is the so-called "step-up" instrument. Unless the student is a music major with rich parents, it should be quite adequate through high school and college, or even to play as an amateur for life, or until he itches for one nicer or classier. Nowadays we can provide a handsome and functionally excellent violin for *well under* a thousand dollars, or a cello for *well under* two thousand. These are new beautifully finished and good sounding instruments, not heavy clunkers. We occasionally sell nice older instruments for up to several thousands, but try to avoid consignment hassles. (I have a grand Strobel cello available now for $17,500 but it is top professional quality.)

More on Pricing

It has been said that violin prices are made of a

rubbery material that stretches to fit any situation. In fact this is true of most "merchandising." That is not true in our "real world violin shop," but some flexibility is always required.

Many shops give 100% credit on trade-in of a violin purchased there off the price of a more expensive instrument. Obviously the price of the new item must be high enough to cover the additional costs of reselling the old one plus a reasonable profit.

I am not educated in business or economics, but here are some points on various pricing definitions as we use them for inexpensive commodity type instruments.

Basic net cost in supplier's catalog

MSRP (manufacturer's suggested retail price) if any, in their catalog = our **list price** for simple items with no value added in our shop, e.g. strings, cases)

Adjusted net cost = instrument net plus shop setup (labor plus new strings, etc., extraordinary shipping costs - can be high for bass, e.g.)

Adjusted list price for the above - appears on our price tag on the instrument. Typically twice our adjusted cost. This is what the customer pays unless there is a discount or "sale." (We have had a standard 25% discount for cash sales for the last 18 years, effectively sharing the profit 50-50 with the customer. This builds customer volume and loyalty and competes well with direct catalog discounters.)

Rent to own price. This may be the same as our list price, but is usually more to cover the additional management, depreciation, and trade-in expenses. Here it is simply 24 times the monthly rate for a two year contract. This is the price used for new instruments purchased with a trade-in. This often turns out to be on the high side, and we lower it when appropriate.

Our "point of sale." Credit card terminal, convenient forms and brochures. Drawers hold strings, rosin, chinrests, shoulder rests, mutes, miscellaneous supplies. Sales counter to the right displays old instruments under glass.

OFFICE PROCEDURES AND FORMS

Our accounting is complicated enough, although it would be much more so if we had employees with payroll and tax withholding. My sons are our business partners, which has its own complications, but seems better for us. In any case it seems unrealistic to run any sort of business nowadays without a computer. (My friend the veterinarian still seems to manage.) Having been an engineer in a previous life, not to mention being a writer and publisher in the present one, I am at home with computers, and they are in fact a compelling hobby of mine. This is neither necessary nor desirable. If you simply use them well you will waste less time. (But back up your data religiously and keep a copy off site, as in a safe deposit box.)

QuickBooks is the most popular and suitable accounting program for our purposes. It has an optional payroll feature that we don't use, but it has all the business accounting functions needed including accounts, inventory, customer lists, billing, etc. *TurboTax* is used for tax computation and filing. Depending on your kind of business, accounting can be simple or complicated. (It's almost worth moving to Oregon just to avoid the accounting complications of sales tax, as I recall from our California days.) We write off certain small parts like mutes and fine tuners, and bulk items like glue and hair as they are received, but things like strings and shoulder rests, and of course instruments, should be removed from inventory only as they are used.

Every instrument we stock has a unique number on a small piece of white paper that we glue to the inside back through the right soundhole. This provides the owner an identification in case of loss or theft, and provides us a tracking number. All the better bows have a unique number pencilled onto the ivory tip. Place the retail prices with the numbers and name stamps on paper in the bottom of the bow case. This can be easily erased by the buyer if he likes, but provides us an in house stock number. Inexpensive generic bows are not numbered.

Every instrument on display should be tagged with its list price, and whether or not it comes as an outfit. This removes any suspicion of arbitrary pricing, and you can quickly compute a discount in the case of a sale unencumbered by a trade in, etc.

In the last chapter I mentioned how nearly indispensable it was to accept payment by credit or debit cards. We got by without for many years, and you can too in a small simple business. But the advantages are nearly compelling, in spite of the fees (about 3%). We started using credit cards to sell books directly from my website. (The customer sends his credit card information to my secure server using SSL, which then comes to me by encrypted email. We then type it into our credit card terminal.) As soon as we got the terminal we realized how convenient it was to "swipe" customers cards into it in the shop for retail sales. You will probably need a separate telephone line for the terminal, since it has to be available at any time. We decided to get our credit card account through the same bank as our business account. That way the receipts are promptly deposited into our account. You can lease a terminal from the bank but it is much less expensive to buy one. We bought the excellent Nurit 2085 with a built-in printer for about $300 from www.merchantwarehouse.com

Insurance - I am not the right person to advise you about insurance. It can be a complicated, expensive thing. There are many kinds, business, liability, inventory, instruments on loan, malpractice, or a catchall violin shop policy. We know our risks, and are pretty much self-insured. I am not bragging or advising this. We don't handle or work on many really expensive instruments. Our major risks are customers who can't pay their bills, and you can't insure against that!

I suppose it should go without saying that repair bills should be collected before delivery. But for instrument sales or rentals, most shops will have to make some kind of credit sales, and some suggestive sample forms are shown here. I devised them for everyday use in our family violin shop. They are well tested, but have not been checked for legal correctness. Perhaps they might be adapted for use in your business (at least replace my name with yours!) They might not be suitable for larger, more aggressive operations.

The first is a convenient, **general purpose form** for routine shop counter sales as well as repair work orders. Your local quick printer can use 8.5 by 11 in duplicate (or triplicate) carbonless form stock and slice them in two. He can also print serial numbers at additional expense. We find this unnecessary, since many of these forms end up as rough notes and are rewritten. The formal billing of outside accounts and institutions is done with printed invoices in our Quickbooks accounting program.

The **rental forms** are vastly simpler and more liberal than those of many music stores, but this is how we operate. *(Disclaimer: I simply wrote these, you may want to have an attorney check yours.)*

Advertise your assets. Have a **printed handout** available to every visitor to your shop, and include them in mailings, statements, etc. to customers. This should spell out what is better about your shop.

A good **web site** is more and more important. The address should be on every piece of paper you print. So much better if it conveys an international character, depth, strength, and image over and above your local shop impression. You can present behind-the-scenes information, virtual shop tours, photo galleries of your instruments, etc. Look at **www.HenryStrobel.com** for an example.

AFTERWORD

This concludes the main text of the book, although practical examples of business forms follow, and the Appendices, which contain pertinent and interesting readings and a content reference to the other Strobel books.

So some concluding remarks are in order. We moved here over eighteen years ago and through that time have enjoyed and contributed to the top notch school string program that Salem, Oregon is noted for. We can't take this for granted, especially now, with the Bush era economic situation that has put most state and local government budgets on the rocks. We hope that impending cuts to school music programs will not be so deep and long lasting as they might. "Real world violin shops" will be more important than ever in extending the benefits of music for our young people.

This book has been the hardest for me to write. I am not by preference a businessman. It's boring compared to art and craft and music and philosophy. I would not do it at all unless the profit motive were mitigated by the personal contacts and satisfaction of contributing to the common good. This has been a personal book for me and my family in our particular situation. It will not fit everyone. The repair and instrument costs are only "guesstimates." My experience has been limited to our own shop operation. Many businesses would not and could not operate along these lines, profit requirements and overhead considerations overruling. But for many current or aspiring violin repairmen and shop proprietors, I trust this book will be well worth studying.

Thanks to my dear wife, and now to my two sons, without whom I could not (would not) continue this work.

Henry Strobel

(duplicate sales receipt & record)

Henry Strobel, Violin Maker & Publisher

Salem, Oregon's Professional Violin Shop Since 1985 www.HenryStrobel.com

10878 Mill Creek Road, Aumsville OR 97325   Tel. (503) 749-1742

Record Number_____

SALE ☐   WORK ☐   RECEIPT ☐

Month_____ Day_____ Year_____

NAME				P.O.	
ADDRESS				TEL.	

DESCRIPTION OF ITEM OR SERVICE	ITEM NO.	QTY.	EACH	AMOUNT

NOTES: CASH☐ or CARD☐ or CHECK☐ NO. _____

Henry Strobel & Sons Violin Shop

(Henry Strobel, Violin Maker & Publisher)

Service, Selection, Value
in String Instruments

Author/Publisher of Books
& Videos For Violin Makers

Salem, Oregon's Professional Violin Shop since 1985

10878 Mill Creek Road, Aumsville OR 97325 USA

Appt: **(503) 749-1742**   Web: **www.HenryStrobel.com**

(business card)

(yellow pages ad)

Henry Strobel & Sons Violin Shop

10878 Mill Creek Road
Aumsville OR 97325 USA

(Please substitute your own letterhead.)

Henry Strobel & Sons Violin Shop in Oregon since 1985

telephone: (503) 749-1742   fax: (708) 575-5367   books@HenryStrobel.com   www.HenryStrobel.com

RENT-TO-OWN CONTRACT

I understand that the purpose of rent-to-own is to enable a student to try an instrument without initially buying it. I may return it any time to cancel the current contract. Within two years I may trade it in for a second instrument of equal or greater value, subject to stock on hand, by paying the cash difference between my total (current) payments on it and the rent-to-own price of the second instrument. Rent-to-own contracts are based on 24 monthly payments, 2 of which are required in advance. If at any time I choose to pay off the current balance owed, I may deduct 25%.

Subsequent rent-to-own contract(s) may be available for subsequent instrument(s), subject to our approval, with a 10% increase in rent-to-own price. 100% credit is normally given for payments made on the total contract price (see below) of the current instrument being traded-in. Note that this credit may be more or less attractive to you, depending on the term used, etc., and you may wish to discuss alternatives with us.

I understand that I am legally responsible for damage or loss, except ordinary wear. Upon request Henry Strobel will provide normal maintenance free, but will replace broken strings, bows, etc. at list less 25% unless resulting from defects in material or workmanship. If I default on payments I must return the equipment immediately. Failure to return unpaid equipment may result in criminal prosecution and liability for expenses incurred by Henry Strobel in recovery of unpaid equipment such as legal fees, court costs, etc.

Credit card information: (Required for rent-to-own contracts. Otherwise ask us about a discounted cash purchase, which also qualifies for 100% trade-in credit.)

MC( ) Visa( ) Amex( ). No._ _ _ _ - _ _ _ _ _ - _ _ _ _ - _ _ _ _, expires _ _ / _ _ ,

bearing the name (print): _____. If payment is not received by the due

date, I authorize Henry Strobel to charge it to this credit card. I choose one of the following:

( ) Please automatically charge this card on each due date.

( ) I will normally pay by check or cash. Late payments will be applied to the next month(s).

Employer_____ How long?____ Work Phone (_ _ _)_ _ _ _-_ _ _ _

Own home( ) or rent home( )? How long?__)__ Oregon Driver's License _____

Henry Strobel agrees that   Name . . . . _____

                              Address . . . _____

                              City, ZIP . . . _____

                              Phone . . . . (_ _ _)_ _ _ -_ _ _ _

                              Music Teacher _____ School _____ Grade_____

shall rent to own   Instrument no._____Kind_____ Size ____ Notes_____

                              Rent-to-Own Price . . . . $_____

                              Less Trade-in Credit, if any . . . . ($_____)

                              Total Contract Price . . . . $_____

                              Less 2 payments in advance Chk( ) Cash( ) Card( ) . . . . ($_____)

                              Balance Due . . . . $_____

$____ is payable each month in advance beginning on (month)___, (day)___, 2003 until the balance is

paid or this contract is closed by valid return or trade-in.

Date of contract (month)___, (day)___, 2003.   Agreed and signed_____

Need these extras? Book_____, Stand_____, Spare strings____, Metronome/Tuner_____, Mute____, Other_____

(YOUR LETTERHEAD)

Simple Rental Contract

I understand that the purpose of instrumental rental is to enable me to use an instrument without buying it. I may return it at any time to cancel the current contract. I will pay only for the actual time rented, including a partial month, and for any damages beyond ordinary wear. Any prepaid advance or security deposit in excess of that owed will be returned when the instrument is returned. Henry Strobel may terminate this contract after one year. I may terminate it anytime but will be liable for a minimum of two months rent.

I understand that I am legally responsible for damage or loss, except ordinary wear. Upon request Henry Strobel will provide normal maintenance free, but will replace broken strings, etc. at list less 25% unless resulting from defects in material or workmanship. If I default on payments I must return the equipment immediately. My failure to return unpaid equipment may result in criminal prosecution and liability for expenses incurred by Henry Strobel in recovery of unpaid equipment such as legal fees, court costs, etc.

Credit card information: (required for rental contracts)

MC( ) Visa( ) Amex( ). No. _ _ _ _ - _ _ _ _ _ - _ _ _ _ - _ _ _ _ , expires _ _ / _ _ , bearing the

name (print): _____. If payment is not received by the due date, I authorize

Henry Strobel to charge it to this credit card.

( ) Please automatically charge this card on each due date.

( ) I will normally pay by check or cash.

( ) I have paid a security deposit of $ _____ as required by Henry Strobel.

Employer_____ How long?_____ Work Phone (_ _ _) _ _ _ - _ _ _ _

Own home( ) or rent home( )? How long?_____ Oregon Driver's License _____ Henry

Strobel agrees that   Name   .   .   . . _____

                  Address   . . .   _____

                  City, ZIP . . . _____

                  Phone . . . . (_ _ _) _ _ _ - _ _ _ _

                  Music Teacher _____ School _____ Grade_____

shall rent   Instrument no.____Kind_____ Size ____ Notes_____

and pay   2 payments in advance Chk( ) Cash( ) Card( ) . . . . ($_____)

and pay $_____, the replacement value of this equipment immediately if it is lost, or the cost of repairs if damaged.

$____ is payable each month in advance beginning on (month)___, (day)___, 2003 until this contract is closed by valid return.

Date of contract (month)___, (day)___, 200_.   Agreed and signed _____

(YOUR LETTERHEAD)

INSTALLMENT PURCHASE CONTRACT

Henry Strobel agrees that   Name . . . . _____
                                          Address . . . _____
                                          City, ZIP . . . _____
                                          Phone . . . . (___) ___ - ____
                                          Music Teacher _____ School _____ Grade_____

shall purchase   Instrument no.____Kind_____ Size ____ $_____
                                          And_____ $_____
                                          And_____ $_____
                                          And_____ $_____
                                          Total . . . . $_____
                                          Less Trade-in Credit, if any . . . . ($_____)
                                          Less Down Payment Chk( ) Cash( ) Card( ) . . . . ($_____)

                                          Total Installment Balance Due . . . . $_____

$_____ or more is payable each month in advance beginning on (month)___, (day)___, 2003 until the balance is paid.

I understand that the purpose of this installment sale is to allow me to pay with a down payment followed by several installments. This sale has no interest or carrying charges over our agreed prices, nor does it carry any guaranteed trade-in provisions. Our normal warranties apply.

I further understand that I am legally responsible for damage or loss to this equipment until paid for. If I default on payments I must return the equipment immediately. My failure to return unpaid equipment may result in criminal prosecution and liability for expenses incurred by Henry Strobel in recovery of unpaid equipment such as legal fees, court costs, etc.

Credit card information:

MC( ) Visa( ) Amex( ). No. _ _ _ _ - _ _ _ _ - _ _ _ _ - _ _ _ _ , expires _ _ / _ _ , bearing the name (print): _____. If payment is not received by the due date, I authorize Henry Strobel to charge it to this credit card. Subject to Henry Strobel's approval, I choose one of the following options:

( ) Please automatically charge this card on each due date.

( ) I have given you post-dated checks for the balance. I guarantee availability of funds at the due dates.

Employer_____ How long?_____ Work Phone (_ _ _) _ _ _ - _ _ _ _

Purchaser's bank_____ Bank branch address Bank_____

Own home( ) or rent home( )? How long?_____ Oregon Driver's License _____

Date of contract (month)___, (day)___, 2003.   Agreed and signed _____

(YOUR LETTERHEAD)

INSTRUMENT LOAN CONTRACT

I agree to borrow the equipment listed below for evaluation and to buy or return it in the same condition to Henry Strobel on or before ____ / ____ / ____.

I offer the following credit card information as a credit reference and security:

MC( ) Visa( ) Amex( ). No._ _ _ _ - _ _ _ _ _ - _ _ _ _ _ - _ _ _ _ _,

expires _ _ / _ _ , bearing the name (print): _____.

If the equipment is not returned by the due date, I authorize Henry Strobel to charge this credit card.

And / or I deposit $_____ with Henry Strobel in cash or check, to be retained by him in the event I fail to buy or return by the due date above, any additional balance remaining payable.

The borrowed equipment consists of:

Item Name_____   Stock/serial no. _____Price $_____

Item Name_____   Stock/serial no. _____Price $_____

Item Name_____   Stock/serial no. _____Price $_____

Item Name_____   Stock/serial no. _____Price $_____

Total Value of Equipment Lent   . . . . $_____

I further agree that the equipment above is entrusted to my safekeeping and responsibility for buying at the above price(s) or returning in like condition by the due date, and that Henry Strobel has not insured it for loss while in my possession. Failure to return unpaid equipment may result in criminal prosecution and liability for expenses incurred by Henry Strobel in recovery of unpaid equipment such as legal fees, court costs, etc.

Agreed this date ____ /____ / ____.

Name (print)_____, Address _____

Signature _____, Home phone_____ Work phone_____

(Original to Henry Strobel, photocopy to borrower)

APPRAISAL   March 11, 2003

To whom it may concern:

The cello, the identifying photograph(s) of which ares printed onto this document, in the possession of xxxxx yyyyyyyyy of Salem, Oregon, has, in my opinion, a fair market value of $29,000. It is labelled "*Gavinies, rue S. Thomas du Louvre Paris , 1771.*"

This label is quoted for appraisal identification, not certification, and this appraisal may be considered an evaluation update based on the sale price to the current owner of $ 23,000 in 1986. At that time violin expert Dario D'Attili wrote his opinion that it was "French work of the last quarter of the eighteenth century." See his attached certificate of origin.

(signed)

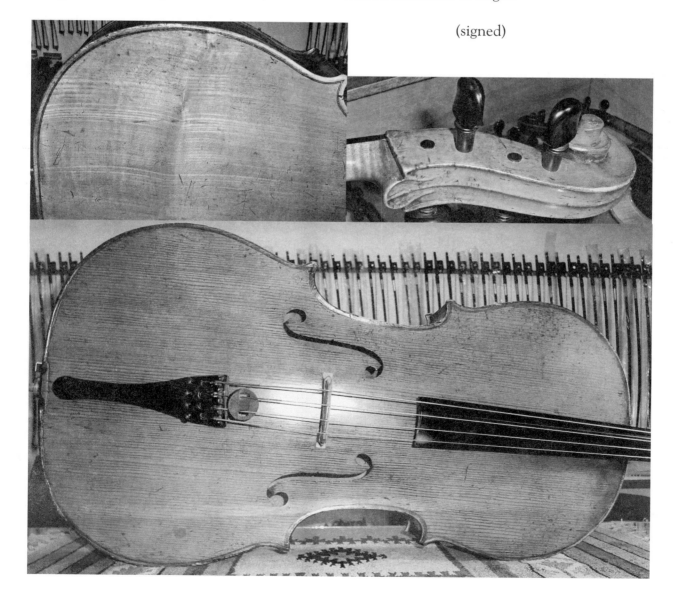

APPENDIX I. SELECTED EMAIL POSTINGS

(See page 21 for an explanation of this material.)

Beginning in January 1995

Thanks for the information and list. This is a lot of work for you and it's greatly appreciated. . . I look forward to sharing information . . .

❧

The correlation between stiffness (E) and hardness is illuminating, but less significant, I think, for soundboards than the ratio of stiffness to density.

Species	E	lb/cu ft	relative stiffness/density
Engelmann	1.28	21.5	.06
White S.	1.34	25	.05
Black S.	1.53	33	.46
Sitka S.	1.57	26.5	.06

According to these data, Engelmann and Sitka are both good front woods, as we know. It would appear that white and black spruce are less desirable, not surprisingly. Experience also corroborates that fronts of Engelmann are made thicker than those of Sitka. I am not convinced that the same figure of merit (stiffness/density) applies to ribs and backs. Here I get better results with more flexible maple. Another factor not considered here is damping, whether flat or frequency dependent. I didn't include red spruce because I didn't have a density figure for it. Ido have some very nice pieces of it that I plan to use. I have not seen white spruce (P. glauca) that I know of.

Mostly I use known wood bought directly from the logger, but have also used "mystery" wood with good results. If it looks and feels right, it likely is.

❧

I think sugar maple and rock maple are the same. About the distinct and even unattractive figure of much acermacrophyllum, especially fast growing "swamp trees", I agree. But some trees are exceptional and lovely, with close, indistinct annual rings. (For an example, see page 76 of my Violin Making, Step by Step.) About the color, why must wood be white? Does it have to look "European"? Chris D. and I have traded Engelmann S. and Oregon Maple in past years. Some European maple cuts much more cleanly, but you can make fine instruments without it.

❧

You obviously assume that "playing-in" is a real factor; I guess we all do to a degree. But that is a large, unquantified subject in itself. Apart from the fact that dealers often tell people buying new instruments that they will improve with a little playing, other factors are the inevitable early "shakedown or break-in" adjustment changes, string changes, etc. Also the adaptation of the player, physical and mental, is at least as important as that of the instrument. (Over the long term, we have regraduation, etc. that may quietly occur. You're not thinking of this, of course, but it, plus natural selection, accounts for the preponderance of old violins that sound better.) In fact not all new instruments need playing-in to sound good. I have made a few violins and cellos that played wonderfully from the first bow touch. Those that did not, I would not expect to improve significantly without the maker's intervention. I presume there is a small change as the varnish matures. And perhaps small changes in the wood and glue joints, but objective data on this would be hard to find.

❧

Kasha bar: Back in the 60's I received . . . a set of guitar designs, including a prepublication piece on acoustics, which also described a notched or double-humped violin bar. (I was never a guitar maker.) I admit I did try the violin bar at the time, but wrote it off as another of those vagaries of the violin. I have seen and/or replaced various odd bars over the years. A couple looked like extreme Cupid's bows. Oh, well.

❧

Chin and shoulder rests: Those who are shop keepers as well as violin makers know the painstaking (painful?) process of matching a violin with a musician. Another such, and less remunerative, area is that of matching a violin to a body. One feels like a shoe salesman. The violin comes in one size, fiddlers in many. I am a mere 6'3", but teenagers frequently are taller nowadays, or at least have pencil necks. "Old school" violinists (usually endomorphs, built like Isaac Stern) still decry the use of these "artificial appliances." Some young violinists, my son among them, find the excellent Kun rests too low, and the Wolf Secondo, with extenders installed, barely high enough.

❧

Your ruminations on "violin acoustics" and "applied science" struck a sympathetic chord with me. Much of what is called violin acoustics is measurement and control, which is important in manufacturing and violin making. Some find such "Chladni tools and rules" invaluable. I do not, and much prefer relying on what I learned from good violins and violinists and traditional makers. (I say this as one educated in physics and an ex engineer.) Of course we've all gained insights from violin research; I'm sure I have from reading the CAS papers over the last 30-40 years. But whatever tools we use, music and violin making are by definition arts. We will not likely make them sciences.

❧

Thanks for the comments on the router setup. It is actually very similar to an experience I had some years ago. I bought an inexpensive fixture from Sears Roebuck (may still be available - called a router-recreater) that worked on similar lines. I could not use it, too much trouble and wouldn't stay put. Things like this have to be heavy duty, and take too much setup time and cost for most of us. (They're essential in factories.) A friend of mine has one by Marlin big enough for cellos, but it's a little bouncy too. I saw Hammond Ashley's big bass router a few years ago, which I'm sure works.

❧

Question on cello neck reinforcement: I still have to repair stuff, and have fixed countless necks broken at the bottom end. You know, the hidden maple dowel. Does anyone make their new cellos (celli if you must) with cross grain reinforcement? I've considered putting in a tapered dowel before assembly. This could make it worse in a really bad accident, but would prevent breaks from lesser shocks. You may also have seen a current popular English how-to book whose author recommends a spline-in-slot reinforcement. I don't know if the cross grain shrinkage differential is a serious problem with seasoned wood. Thanks for all the enlightened remarks on this prosaic problem. Having (re)considered everything, let me try to summarize.

Repairs:
Most reinforcement is done here, since most cellos are not reinforced before. The maple dowel is the best. It practically never fails if done correctly. (I don't think that's begging the question.) Compared with a rectangular spline, it can place more wood in the vital area near the surface at the "L", and does not require complete removal of the neck to install. The dowel is not parallel to the bottom of the neck, but "angled back". I would never use a steel screw; I have seen many such repairs (by others) that failed, letting the old break open partially.

New making:
Tradition notwithstanding, I have considered initial reinforcement. I am doing that on my current cello. Using a tapered rather than a cylindrical dowel is a little more trouble, but fits the shape better and allows a tighter fit (assuming the tapers match).

Cases:
A good "suspension" design is essential for protection in transit and accidents. These support the bottom, not the top of the neck.

. . . wise cautions on dowel insertion: with a blind hole, as in a repair, I use glue escape grooves on the sides of the dowel. And the hole has to be very straight as well as the right diameter. With new construction, before assembly, a small glue release hole could be placed at the bottom of the hole either toward the button or the block. (Or a tapered dowel could perhaps be run right through - not through the button!). Actually it is unnecessary and probably undesirable to put the tapered dowel all the way through; most breaks occur toward the top, and this would be limited by the reamers available. An ordinary cello peg reamer would be too narrow at the top end, for instance. (The standard use of cylindrical dowels in neck repairs is treated in Weisshaar's book and in Art & Method of the Violin Maker by one Strobel.)

❧

. . . asked about reconciling the color of Oregon maple with white Engelmann spruce. I sponge on a dilute water stain to match the colors. JOHA natural water stain no. 423 or GEWA 464.004 gives a "salmon" color overall. This is sealed with a colorless, thin spirit varnish, followed by a yellow oil varnish. The result is a golden ground on which to apply the colored varnish proper (oil or spirit). This process is described in detail in my 5th book "Violin Making, Step by Step." I an now writing Cello Making, Step by Step" and am using a 1-piece back of Oregon maple and an Engelmann front. My maple tree is, I guess, Acer macrophyllum, (I only saw the log, not the leaves) but is different than the usual, having narrow, close, indistinct annual rings and an exquisite figure on the quarter or the slab. The color is the typical. Some pieces of Sitka Spruce match it quite well. I have usually considered color in wood an asset, part of the work already done. I probably should say something, being the perpetrator of the advice to stain bare wood. Yes, I am well aware of and have advised several places in print of the problems of excessive or uneven stain. I was speaking here of a very light stain, and I have no problems of grain reversal, etc. like the Nüssbaum (walnut shell) stained German examples. And I certainly don't recommend the use of potassium bichromate stain, which has additional problems. Interestingly the Hammerls, in "Violin Varnish", page 122, in what is a rather poor translation - I don't have the original - say: "In contrast to stain 422 (largely a Kcl solution), stain 423 consists of natural pigments dissolved in water. As a result, the stain does not spot when applied to wood. (Especially if pre- dampened.) The parenthetical comments are mine. I have a strong aversion to putting stuff like eggs or glue under my varnish, although I am well aware of this Mittenwald practice, which Hammerl also recommends. Water should remove glue, not varnish, in my opinion. And I guess their indices of refraction are not optimum.

The poisonous character of potassium bichromate is certainly one of its "additional problems" that I had in mind. (Others are selective wood staining and long term color and chemical changes.) There are a number of common shop substances that are hazardous, and I tried to identify them in the "Shop Safety" chapter in "Violin Maker's Notebook". Based on the discussion it seems this one was treated with insufficient gravity there, although I had noted that it was "poisonous and perhaps unnecessary" a few pages before. I always feel uncomfortable using it, and carefully keep the solution off my fingers. Most shops probably buy the neck stain solution and never see the much more hazardous orange powder. Inhalation of the dust of several powdered metallic pigments is also unhealthy. Better to use the "readymix." Common sense is good too.

The English frog name, nut, is not Francophobe but from the eyelet (a nut), the female counterpart of the screw. Further, the OED notes that nut has been applied to a plethora of things, including male counterparts. I hope this discussion has reached its nadir.

Just a brief clarification of what I said about oils. I've never used and don't recommend linseed oil as an acoustic ground, i.e in the corpus, or even the thick oil varnish grounds used commonly to "fire" the wood. However, linseed oil can be recommended for use in finishing the neck. But I would never put a non drying (mineral) oil into any part of the wood. As a ground proper I use a thin, shallow spirit varnish to seal the wood without undo penetration.

More participants and broader views. This forum can perform a real service to the profession by sharing information and providing consultation to its members. It can help junior people or those without the benefit of professional education to avoid reinventing the wheel - or crashing the vehicle. So it's good to be frank and clear when controversial (not to say wrong) proposals are made. Some things are so much a part of standard professional practice, and for good reasons, that departures should not be overlooked. If someone wants to make his own violin with Titebond or Elmer's glue, OK, I guess. But I would be most unhappy if someone repaired my instrument (or bow) with same. (Sure, white glue is OK for the leather grip.) Hot glue has been superseded for bow repairs by specialized epoxies or cyanoacrylates, but it remains the right (normally the only) choice for the fiddle for stability, reversibility, and other reasons. If a neck joint fails, it is not because good hot glue was used, unless it was exposed to

extremes of heat and/or humidity.
. . . A drying oil, e.g. linseed, might be used as a ground. But we would not "Pennzoil" our violin in the white. In fact many luthiers use water rather than oil sharpening stones to avoid the possibility of mineral oil contamination. . . I use cyanoacrylates in bow repairs. Some, e.g. Loctite 411, are quite strong and not excessively fast in setting, although that does depend on the surrounding chemistry. I had been looking for higher temperature resistant epoxies, and I mention one odd thing I ran across, an epoxy made by Ciba-Geigy, Araldite TDR 1100-11, "formulated for bonding glass laminates, wood, and plastic components in the construction of ARCHERY BOWS." I have not tried it.

1996
Dear David, the viola drawings arrived today. Special delivery at that. Thanks very much! The drawings are interesting to study. The back is apparently wider in the middle than the front. I guess this might give some clues to (Andrea) Guarneri's assembly sequence, given other data. And either the ribs were not quite vertical or the front and back were different as well as asymmetrical, which I think you mentioned. (My earlier book got a rather grumpy review in the Galpin Society Journal. The reviewer basically said that such asymmetry rules out any original geometric design. I think that the instrument designs as such are essentially symmetrical even though individual instruments are not. My fiddles are crooked even though my templates are symmetrical.) . . .

Poplar is much more acceptable to players in a viola or cello than a violin, and can work very well in them. It may be softer and less strong, so you might want to compensate for this. For example, I put bushings in the pegholes right away for better durability there.

Just returned from a wonderful weekend In San Diego. Norman Pickering, Bill Fulton, and I gave presentations at the bi-annual symposium of the Southern California Association of Violin Makers. It was about the pleasantest violin meeting I've ever been to. The mountaintop campus of the University of San Diego with its mission architecture and beautiful gardens made it more of a retreat. Good friends, food, facts, and music. Even Mrs. Strobel, who is usually not wild about violin conventions, liked this one.

I thought I would have nothing more to say on this subject (Engelmann), but I just was talking with real world wood expert Bruce Harvie, and these are some of his observations, if I can recall and paraphrase them correctly: The first thing is not to generalize, since this wood is very variable. He feels that back in the 70's when harvesting Engelmann from standing dead trees was in vogue, some of the wood was not of the best quality, and might have suffered from the exposure. (But again not to generalize, since he has recently got some excellent wood from a dead stand in Montana.) He thinks that the Engelmann he is harvesting from live trees is very sturdy wood, as well as very difficult to distinguish microscopically from "European spruce. End quote.

This struck a chord with me. Bob Scoville, who moved later to Corte Madera, then Cotati, CA was/is a good friend of mine, and I too got Engelmann spruce from him about that time. I last saw him at the VSA in Oakland. David Bromberg and I both learned some things in his shop.

. . . what I object to in some of the varnish and technique "discoveries," the implication that if you are not doing it this way, the way the "Old Italians" did it, of course, you are doing it inferiorly. This begs the question in several ways: that the Old Italian ways were best, that the Old Italians were consistent, that this or that was in fact the way(s) they did it. Someone who took seriously the violin "literature" over the years might conclude that the old makers must have been very busy or very confused if they did all the things they have been charged with. What is more to the point is whether we are making artistic instruments (tools) that artists like, buy, and use for the long term. Whatever material or technique (old or new) is used to achieve this, we need not always find validation by antecedent in the old makers. Who I suppose didn't use Engelmann spruce either. :-)

*

Some varnish looks better, some violins sound better, and most will agree on the grosser perceptions. But much of the inner fire and some of the nuances of sound are subjective, and also depend significantly on the light and the acoustics. Years ago, I was shown an "interesting" violin, purportedly a Strad that had been secluded in Ireland for "centuries." I took it out into the bright sun, and immediately I was taken by the "inner fire." In fact, many old dull looking violins sparkle in the bright sun. And we know how differently violins sound in the studio or in the auditorium (and depending on who plays them). We now know that antique violins have no essential priority in varnish or (obviously) workmanship, or in sound, when fairly compared. Witness recent old vs. new cello tone trials. Old violins ARE different; they have more years, and whatever of selection, memory, history, rarity, care, originality, association etc. goes with those years. And they cost more.

*

About the recent discussion of the protective barrier between the casting plaster and the varnish, I have always used the thin plastic film used in the kitchen. (At least for routine partial casts.) Of course it has to be stretched smooth with tape to avoid wrinkles. I do not really care for the method that coats the varnish with mineral oil under pressure.

*

Yes, there's no magic here; all such "extracts" (liquid colorants) fade to a degree in oil varnish in the sun, some more than others. One has to compensate by overcoloring. I used this method in the book because it is easy for beginners to apply. Spirit varnish is of course the easy way to color, and lakes and glazes provide some success with oil, but I had a friend, Roger O'Donnell, now deceased, who occasionally used water based varathane, and took advantage of the very permanent rainbow of water soluble dyes. A green violin (a salute to his ancestors?) hung on his wall. I recently used this varnish (uncolored) on a floor, but do not plan to use it on fiddles.

*

. . . about the ribs. Unless of course there is something special about them, as when they are made of the kind of wood that I have been describing in recent postings, in which the amplitude of the curl is great compared with the thickness of the ribs, which makes them much less stiff than typical and gives them more damping, and that periodically anisotropic. (Of course I doubt the last is important, but it could be increased somewhat by a soft varnish penetrating into the "end grain".) I don't like to brand the observations of working violin makers as "folklore" even if not well quantified. Terms such as "stifling tone" are fair language among violin makers if not Whitehead and Russell. That damping behavior is roughly similar in maple and spruce is perhaps a generalization that might be taken with a grain of salt in certain cases. In any case, I must say that I have read your papers over the years and always been impressed. I usually read and write these things at 6:00AM so please be kind in pointing out any non sequiturs.

*

. . . I forgot to mention that my flexible ribs were of the usual thickness, not thinned down. The wood characteristics I think made the difference. Some years ago I had to do a lot of corpus repairs to a striking cello; the advanced student who played it loved the back inlays of birds and flowers, but it was a very dead cello, and he now has a real one. Anyway, what I noticed most was that this old handmade cello had very thick laminated ribs, and indeed someone had doubled them all for strength.

*

Well, I am of course not a disinterested judge. Like everyone, I tend to use what works for me, what I am comfortable with. Getting a decent varnish is pretty much a matter of care and experience. The main method I described in the book was chosen for ease and practicality, but looks fine, too. I will have, in the next week or so, IF we get any sun here, a fiery photo on my home page of the cello I have just finished varnishing. The varnish I used here is very ordinary, but good, and dries practically overnight. I don't think there's merit per se in doing things the hard way. It's Hammerl's standard oellack, as sold currently by Vitali,

for example, colored with Hammerl's brown "extract" (which I got via GEWA about 30 years ago). Probably still the same. My grounding is a little different (wrong according to some), never glue or gelatin, usually a light spirit varnish sealer, excess wiped off with an alcohol cloth. The other thing difference is that I first (yes) sponge a dilute Hammerl organic water stain onto the bare wood. This has a salmon color when dry. Then the previously mentioned spirit sealer, then a coat of yellow oil varnish, which, over the water stain gives a nice golden undertone. Over this the color coats, which can be modified, if you like, with different colors, subtle glazes, etc. (I don't use any glaze in this straight method.) Before all these applications, I rub with appropriate grades of 3M "Scotchbrite" type mild abrasive pads. Starting out with beautiful wood is the most important. The varnish is never more than handmaiden to the wood.

*

Nussbaum is of course German for walnut tree, also the wood, nuts, their hulls, and the brown-black stain obtained from them. Beize is German for stain. As a boy in Indiana I became very familiar with this stain as I harvested black walnuts. Unlike the English walnuts (which also have this stain, but less intense), the American walnuts had very hard shells, best opened with a hammer, and deeply stained fingers were common. Kremer's catalog offers "walnut hulls, cut pieces." I guess this dark stain (used on the wood) is what turned the spruce grain negative on some old German violins. I never tried it for crackle, but I'm sure some of the Weisshaar alumni could elaborate. I have had a light pretty, crackle develop over time when I used spirit over oil varnish.

*

I might also say that these last violas were made approximately on the model of the late Louis Kievman's excellent small Gasparo da Salo viola, which he showed me at the VSA convention in Chicago a dozen or so years ago.

*

This is getting philosophical. May as well get my oar in, too. Color (subjective) is the light we see - hue, brightness, etc. Color (objective) is a property of the varnish the artist (maker) paints on. The photographer is a painter whose varnish is light. (photos - graphein). He also controls what we see by lighting it. Recent comments lucidly relevant. We can illuminate selectively, clarifying, showing, emphasizing some truths about the object, downplaying (concealing?) others, as epitomized in portrait photography. What is the truth we want to show to the eyes of the camera, the reader, the customer (the patron of the art)? Examples: 1. To emphasize the wood flame we use a single, distant (collimated) light, like the sun, not flat, multiple lighting, which conceals curl. 2. We would not want to display an unfortunately red fiddle in incandescent light any more than we would want to varnish or retouch or photograph in such light. So we can manipulate color as maker or photographer or presenter. There is yet another level of control, a post paint brush available to the photographer (photo-retoucher) and publisher. Most prepress (even mine) now comes from the computer. In addition to changing brightness, contrast, hue, perspective, etc., we can easily add or subtract a tattoo or a knothole. While the human eye automatically compensates to a degree for lighting conditions, it does not usually overlook a pimple, except in love (which may apply to violins). What is the truth of color, the color of truth? In what light do we want to see or show our things, ourselves? It was very early in the morning that I wrote this.

*

```
              ---           ---           ---
  /// \\\     /// \\\       /// \\\
------------------------------------------------------------- <-
  ///    \\\   ///   \\\    ///    \\\   \
  ///    \\\   ///   \\\    ///    \\\
                                                    Thickness
                                                    of back
  //     \\\  ///      \\\ ///     \\\   /
------------------------------------------------------------- <-
      \\\ ///      \\\ ///       \\
       ---          ---
```

This shows another kind of repetitive runout found in backs with a high curl amplitude, which can be found in wonderful sounding instruments. What we may think is desirable in front wood - high stiffness to density and damping - is probably not best for backs and ribs. I have used a tree with grain as above in several large and small instruments. Universally, the professional violinists and cellists who tried them remarked on the huge tone and responsiveness. You may be sure that bending back plates (to gain stiffness) has no attraction for me. Some shops are known to scrape ribs thinner on "valuable" violins (modern Italian clunkers for example), to wake them up. In all this, I think the greater flexibility is more significant than the lowered mass. In fact the ribs made of this wood are substantially weaker, which is a potential drawback if an accident occurs, but I think the tone advantage overrides this.

૨►

Steel bows . . . were made by Heddon (the fishing rod company, I guess). They are listed in my 1952 Wm. Lewis and Son catalog. They cost from $7.50 to $15, depending on the fittings and paint job - the "wood grain" ones were $15. I have two (plain brown) in good playing condition, but there must be plenty of them around; they are nearly indestructible (and don't burn).

૨►

I am not playing a game. I like violins - that's why I do it for a living, and I need to know what works. If we are successful, we find out, as far as we can, what works for us. Violin making remains an art, I am happy to find. I have followed much of the research that has appeared in various violin journals for the past 25-30 years, since Ernest Wild, late renowned violin maker of San Francisco, gave me his small file of Catgut Newsletters. He was not enthusiastic about them then, and I personally must conclude that the pickings have not been over rich in the meantime, in terms of generally applicable breakthroughs. Well, having despatched that unpopular, benighted, point of view, I hope folks are still friendly. (Incidentally, I am not a Luddite; I majored in physics, and was a successful electronic engineer in a prior life.)

This forum is a wonderful, but more difficult mode of communication than I had realized. Facetiousness and nuances in conversation can get filtered out. . . . I am not an academic type or a scientist or an original thinker, although I have worked at all those things. I hope to be a philosopher one day. Meantime I still rehair bows, which I am told builds character. At least it keeps my customers congenial. My admittedly jaded reaction to some of the varnish talk is predicated on my long exposure to a lot of it. Omitting the visual rhapsodizing of Charles Reade and the exaggerated tonal importance given varnish by the Hills and others (these were before my time), we have seen a surfeit of "scientific" solutions to what is probably not a secret recipe, or at least not a single one.

૨►

The violin continues to mystify (me anyway). Yesterday I mined an ancient violin out of the back room and fitted it up, hoping to perhaps put it to some use. It had a short "banjo" neck and "built on the back" blockless ribs. The front looked a little thick and had a short bar of triangular section. I was not hopeful of tone, but put a baroque fingerboard on it and tried. This unlikely creature has the most exquisite sound and pleasurable playing characteristics I could desire. I have run into this kind of thing a number of times -- violins which (appear to) break the mold as far as graduation and design are concerned, and threaten to make me despair of understanding the rules. This became the cherished baroque violin of my son's teacher. Yes the violin laughs at us. And in a way, I'm glad it does. Of course I know the laws are consistent, but the rules will not be simple to state.

૨►

I just observed the following. I used a padded spring clamp to stop the 1st position 3rd finger D on the A string with no possibility of touching the E string. A "squeal" was easily reproduced by light, transverse, down bowing at the lower end of the fingerboard, crossing from the A to E string. I admit that this is not "normal" bowing. (My wife, on hearing this, was heard to remark to my son, "He must be doing "research" again.") A similar squeal occurred when the E string was additionally stopped with a fingernail near the nut. I do not have a spectrum analyzer, and do not trust my ear in this range. I think I will go have breakfast now. (I did this

test to exclude the seriously suggested cause of the whistle as merely the string brushing against a errant finger.)

When I went out into the shop later I found dozens of fiddles that would reliably whistle (I like that word better than squeal) sustainably on the E. Most violinists are more or less aware of this occurrence, I think, but don't dwell on it. This has been discussed at various times in the past, with no definitive analysis, and no complete remedy (that I'm aware of.) Why does it seem to occur on down bows but not up bows? . . . My musical son came into the shop this morning to practice. He said "Oh, that's not a note, it's just a squeak." When I detuned the E string he said," It's the same." Could the difference between up and down bows be related to the rapid heating and change in rosin stickiness at the bowing point observed by Norman Pickering in The Bowed String? This is one difference I can think of, i.e. that on the down bow the rosin has just been "used" on the A string, whereas on the up bow it is fresh and cool. Just thinking out loud. The book also treats various aspects of the start up of string vibrations that are relevant to the present discussion, including torsional vibrations. (Which is what are suspected here.) . . . I Krazy-glued (the end of) a 15 mm long piece of horsehair perpendicular to the middle of the E string to try to observe the torsional vibrations. They were clearly evident in normal vibration, but the whistle was gone! I trimmed the hair to about 10 mm, and could again provoke the whistle mode, although less easily, but the torsional vibrations were (apparently) still evident. I then shortened the hair to 5 mm, and it was more prone to whistle, but I the hair was too short to see much. When I cleaned off the hair and glue, the whistle returned with its original vigor. (I'm not making this up.) (Suggestive of Heisenberg's uncertainty principle, where the observance affects the observed?)

૨►

The spline is, I think, the repair of choice for a split off head. It is honest and strong. Cross-grain (of course) pernambuco is good where we want a repair unseen by the casual observer but still easily visible on inspection. Now to my point: I have done not a few splines using a sheet of phenolic insulating material from an old electrical panel. This stiff material is about 0.031 in or 0.8 mm thick, tan in color, but appears to be laminated with a darker center. Used for splines, it looks very handsome, unobtrusive with sort of a "purfled" look (which might be inappropriate on an antique bow, but at least will keep the repair from being overlooked by a buyer). I don't think any of these has failed. I use the thick Loctite cyanoacrylate. In this age of electronics, I am sure several such suitable and convenient materials are available. (In splines the repairer has to be a sculptor too or the lines of the head can be lost.)

૨►

I often wonder at the valuation of violins by violinists and dealers. I was just putting a bridge on a "modern Italian", an Oreste Candi, for a young student, who complained of its being "squeaky." Indeed it was prettily carved although with a trench-like channel, but with a poor thin tone, doubtless the result of its overly robust back and a front that was 4 mm in too many places. To me, this was never a good violin, although it might be made into one by a graduating dealer, and parlayed via the magic Italian name into a profit of not a little. The value-added approach. . . Had this violin not been in her family for years, it would have been regraduated long ago, and hopefully rightly.

૨►

It's a sunny afternoon today, and to refresh my visual memory, I took several dozen new and old bows outside, put my "Optivisor" on and studied the wood appearance. All these bows were definitely considered pernambuco, and most had the characteristic "pebbles in rows" grain. But some (and some of the better ones) had little if any of this appearance, or at least it was rather indistinct. I suppose that this difference followed a difference in subspecies? (Of course none of these were the "Brazilwood" of the common German bows that you mentioned. Referring to my old notes, I seem to have surmised that such were "beefwood" or manilkara bidentata.) One sometimes sees wood that is probably not pernambuco, but still good bow wood. Snakewood of course, but others, as in some decent prewar Nippon bows. I have a bow by Albert Karr of a very stiff squiggly grained different wood. Looked him up in Wenberg: "During

World War II the U.S. government requested that he make bows, and his dairy (in Independence MO) was converted into a bow-making factory. Reported to have produced in excess of one million commercial grade bows, which were machine made, in a six month period. The government purchased these bows, and it has not been determined where they were distributed." I'm not making this up, and I presume Tom wasn't. I doubt that many of these bows were much good, and those that I have seen all had shiny, warped plastic frogs. Maybe these are analogous to the Jackson-Guldan violins? I do think it would be good if someone could tie down some of this wood appearance data in photomicrographs and, if possible, correlate it to species, etc. We rarely get the chance to identify the wood in our bows (or woodpiles) by studying its leaves! Identification (from microstructure) is unreliable, but better information would help. Wood of the same species but in different trees and different parts of the same tree all may vary in mechanical properties, so measuring those is the last word, but it's also nice to know its name.

1997

The only sure way is to try the violin on the child. With the chin on the rest, the fingers of the left hand should be just able to comfortably curl around the end of the scroll. The bow size goes with the violin of course. Violin sizes are not standard. A Suzuki may differ from a German size, for example. Some companies sell a sizing stick to be used with their violins. Most kids start in our schools at 3rd or 4th grade on a 1/2 size.

*

I don't know that anyone ever claimed that the Golden Section had any acoustic significance per se. It had a strong aesthetic and perhaps mystical appeal at the time the violin was designed. That it may be observed, at least approximately, in most violins, is probably because it is inherent (by definition) in the drawing of tangent arcs from the acute angles of a 2:1 right triangle, which is conveniently and typically used now, and I think was originally used in drafting the classic violin shape. A draftsman may also (implicitly) employ the G.S. without (explicitly) knowing it; we can still note it in analysing the design. I have kept my own geometric analyses simple enough for me to understand, and anyone to use, so they may be oversimplified.

*

Rehairing bows is not one of my favorite activities, but it goes along with having customers. I was just removing piecewise a (glued in) head plug with my 3mm chisel when I heard that grating, dulling, sound as it struck a wire wrapping. *@#&* Happens all too often, this unnecessary use of wire ties, but I was surprised . . . to see it given respectability in another new book.

*

When I started repairing cellos, one of the first things I did was to make a support in which the cello could be freely rotated in a horizontal position. It was mainly used to place the cello in a convenient attitude for touch-up, rotate it and work on the other side without waiting for the touch-up to dry. A wide board to lie on the bench with narrow vertical boards attached on both ends. Like a wide "U." One of these end uprights accepts the end pin with a wingnut operated clamp to stop it at any rotation angle. If the end pin is not yet installed (as in varnishing) insert a tapered dowel, which would normally be done as a varnishing aid anyway. The middle of the neck simply rests in an oversized U-shaped notch lined with thick felt. Lightweight, cheap, and very lo-tech. (French polish the neck later.) (But I don't use it anymore - a piece of carpet on the bench seems to suffice.)

*

There have been, I'm sure, millions of these (Glasser fibreglass) bows made, an unbreakable, affordable boon to young students. Mr. Glasser told me there is one in the Smithsonian. As far as I know, his son Andrew is still running the old factory in the Bronx.

*

Someone: "I've also noticed that the A. Guarneri "Primrose" contralto viola is strung so that its C string goes to the highest bass side peg also. Interesting. Any thoughts as to why?" All us old-timers are familiar with this practice, which harks back to the days of fat, fragile C's that didn't take well to a sharp bend down toward the peg. . . I usually turn the wrong peg at first.

*

Don't recall if this method was mentioned, but (like many others I guess) I mark the purfling groove under the back button by placing a strip of purfling in the groove on both sides, bridging it over the central area and adjusting it by eye, then marking with the knife. (Assumes purfling of uniform characteristics, of course.)

*

. . . It is very hard to generalize about brand quality of carbon steel tools because, as you say, it can vary from time to time. In addition to the sources already mentioned, I might mention Frank Mittermeier, Inc. in New York. (718) 828-3843. I recently got a couple of good gouges there, one a 50 mm for cello roughing (had to make a handle for it). These have the "screw" stamp, as well as the "Dastra FM" stamp, and are apparently made by David Strassman Co. "Since 1835." Not fancy, but certainly good enough. . . . You can't tell the edge-holding characteristics of a tool by looking at it or a catalog. I have encountered some awful examples that resisted my best efforts at rehardening and tempering. Over a long time, I have acquired or "inherited" a lot of tools. Only a very few select ones find a place a place on my bench, and these are of varying age, style, and source. The others are thrown away or end up in the attic. The violin maker is almost by occupation a tool-making animal to some degree or should be. All at least make ad hoc jigs and fixtures. I've made a number of special tools, and I guess that the most common shop-made edge tool is the peg shaper. These made with thick, oil-hardening jointer blade stock are far superior to flimsy commercial models. My "multi-holer" can be seen in a photo on page 63 Violin Making Step by Step. The Japanese tools are a little different. Soft stones, planes and saws that pull, and a layering approach to hardened steel blades. (I think the pull cut, in particular, is very appropriate for thin saws.)

*

Dear friends, I had a nice day yesterday and would like to tell you about it. Closed shop and drove to Portland where I spent much of the day learning from generous associates how to cook a nice golden brown varnish and eating apple pie with espresso. After returning, I had a surprise evening visit from a friend, who happens to be my wood cutter, and who was returning from an estate auction with boxes of violins, molds, and violin parts. I immediately bought one of the violins, labeled Wm. Arbuckle, Glasgow, 1895. I had long been looking for a nice souvenir Scottish violin for my personal collection, mainly because I spent three wonderful years in Ayrshire in the early 60's as an air force officer. (The one I had brought back with me at that time was inadequate and was an additional impetus for making my own first violin.) Well, this is a wonderfully made instrument, with some of the cleanest, crispest, work I have seen. Arbuckle, however does not appear in Honeyman or in Henley, and I wonder if someone has further particulars. I know there is a new book out on British makers, and perhaps someone who has it (I do not yet.) could check it for me. Also, among the "parts" was a violin back labelled Justin Gilbert, Victoria, B. C., p.17, 1920. Of course I have his famous book, "Cremona Violin Technique" of 1937. (In fact, my copy is No. 116, inscribed to Mr. Edw Lavendar (earlier of the Strad) with compliments of Justin Gilbert.) I doubt that "p. 17" is related, but on a whim I turned to page 17 of his book, and found what struck me as a remarkable coincidence, da capo, a recipe for cooked varnish, different, but with some definite similarities to what we had been cooking earlier in the day! It always seems to me so natural and unremarkable for early artisans to cook up (simply) a (complex) varnish from any of many vegetable resins and oils, or to dissolve them in suitable spirits, that we hardly need look to Michaelman, et al for answers. Pending further evaluation, I may discuss yesterday's process, and, in the meantime, I will be happy to post the old Gilbert varnish pages, if any evidence interest.

*

It always seems to me so natural and unremarkable for early artisans to cook up (simply) a (complex) varnish from any of many vegetable resins and oils, or to dissolve them in suitable spirits, that we hardly need look to Michaelman, et al for answers. Well, this was just a conversational take from my general impressions of violin "varnishology." I simply don't have the expertise, time, or inclination to debate points about so squishy a subject as violin varnish, any more than violin acoustics. Too many others have done that, generally fruitlessly. But let me try to explain what I meant (conjectured). I guess that the "early artisans" (ancient Egyptians or what have you onward, not thinking specifically of the Sherwin Williams of Cremona), made satisfactory varnishes, cold and hot, suitable for their purposes, but without requiring anything as non-intuitive as Joseph Michaelman's method, even were it suitable. The varnish artisans may have been specialists, probably necessary for quality control of simple but careful production, and thus I suppose many luthiers got theirs from the drugstore. And, as we and other artists do, added thinners, driers, retardants, colors, etc. to taste. The specifics of the application, "color and layering" details, etc. were of overriding importance. Production of pretty and permanent colorants is a potentially huge subject, but I see no reason why the color, especially in the age of the lute or the Fuesseners, was not simply developed in the pot, from heat and/or iron, if not from added artists' colors. (Art historians in this area may find me quite wrong; I look for light and would welcome it.) Makers have sent me samples of what appear to be perfectly adequate varnish of various nice colors cooked up from resins of pines, larch, Douglas fir, balsam, etc., or even, or especially, from rosin, which itself represents merely a step in a cooking process. I have made very little varnish myself, generally considering it unnecessary, albeit a frequent element in a maker's mystique. I consider the Cremona varnish subject roughly analogous to the Cremona tone subject. ;-)

Several have asked me for Justin Gilbert's varnish recipe, and I think that this short excerpt from his book, Cremona Violin Technique, Copyright 1937 by Justin Gilbert, International Copyright 1937, will be acceptable under the "fair use" policy. PLEASE NOTE: This material was only brought up as part of an interesting coincidence related at the beginning of this thread. I have not used and do not plan to use this recipe, nor do I endorse the book in general, which, in my opinion, contains both good as well as questionable advice. It is placed here only as one example of many in the literature. (Strictly FOR WHAT IT IS WORTH) "Here is one recipe which, according to my tests, fulfills all the conditions with respect to one of the old Italian varnishes, proved through all five human senses. It is inexpensive, and perfectly serviceable. Of course, it will be vigorously condemned by certain people, just as any recipe whatever would be condemned. Take rosin, the by-product of turpentine manufacture (the same material as Venetian turpentine), boil it without any lid on the vessel till it is reduced in weight to something like one-third of the original weight (which may take half an hour or several hours, according to the degree of heat) : this darkens its color, necessitating less pigment as coloring, also causing the varnish to dry faster. This resin will make varnish a little too soft: it requires the addition of a hard resin. So take gum copal one part and this reduced rosin two parts, pulverize the gum copal and then fuse it with the resin by heat. The metal vessel used must have a size of, say, four or five times the bulk of the resins put into it, for there will be effervescing while the two resins are fusing. Do not put a cover on the vessel. The heat must be applied by gas flame which you can regulate: for if you allow the material to effervesce over the top of the vessel it will catch fire, and perhaps set fire to the shop. So watch it continually, and turn off extra heat. Have a metal cover for the vessel so that in case of accident by fire you may at once turn out the gas and instantly clap the cover over the top of the vessel: that will smother out any fire in the vessel. You will be unable to fuse copal in oil, therefore it is necessary to first fuse it with the resin, as explained. Now this fusion of resins should be pulverized, weighed, and placed in the vessel for making varnish. Then add equal weight of boiled linseed oil. You can buy it ready boiled: but boil it yourself a little more, for that will make the varnish dry better-if boiled too much it will not fuse with the resins. however. Weigh your empty vessel, put in your pulverized resin mixture. Weigh again to ascertain the weight of resin, then add this re-boiled oil to equal weight of resin, the vessel being large enough for expansion of four or five times the bulk of this material, as in the former case, to allow for fusing. Then add your oil coloring and fuse these three together at the same time. Choose

the color you want from those oil paints that fuse with varnish without leaving any sediment, Windsor- Newton's products, for instance, that are sold in tubes for artists-they do not all fuse in varnish, but instructions will tell you the ones that do. It is oil colors that fuse in oil. For yellow varnish you can choose chrome yellow: a pinkish light red for background, crimson lake; dark red, magenta; brown, vandyke. also burnt umber, etc.-of course, any other colors that you fancy. For strong coloring the amount of the oil coloring should be about one-eighth the weight of the resins, or oil---one-sixteenth the combined weight of the two. Be careful in fusing. Do not try to do it on a stove or over any flame that is not instantly adjustable and instantly put out in case of danger. Stir during the fusing: lessen the heat before the effervescing gets too high: continue till the effervescing ceases, and then do not cook the varnish any more; remove it away from fire, and allow it to partially cool before adding turpentine: add turpentine a little at a time (for there will be more effervescing of hot varnish at first) until the bulk is in- creased by about four times, or until the varnish is thin enough to work with. More turpentine may be stirred in cold. Do not attempt to mix two colors together in the varnish. The mixture of the colors is to be done by successive coats applied to the violin. So do not mix two colors of varnish together to get some certain color: it is not so rich and beautiful and dichromic as you get by applying the different colors in successive coats. When your color is entirely fused in the varnish there will be no residue settling down, and no need to filter. This varnish dries so slowly that it should be dried in the sun; suspending the violin on a short string, first from one end and then the other. Placed out of doors, it will turn around in the wind and expose all parts to the sun; or you can place it on a window sill and when one side is dry expose the other side. Each coat must be absolutely dry before the next is put on; if not the varnish will crack later on. Do not expose your very last two coats to the sun, however, as precaution against cracking afterwards. One or two days will dry a coat in the sun. Apply varnish with thin coats, and rub down each coat when dry with the finest glass-paper obtainable, first rubbing boiled linseed oil over the surface of the glass-paper. Rub off the oil thoroughly with a cloth before applying the next coat. Then when the last coat is on, and has been allowed to dry indoors, wrap a soft cloth over a flat piece of art-gum or rubber, apply raw linseed oil to this, and use this to rub down the varnish with powdered pumice stone. Finish off with something still finer, like tripoli or rotten stone. Note that you use raw linseed oil now, instead of boiled oil. Raw linseed oil is used as a preventive of cracking. It is the proper dressing for this kind of varnish. There should be one or two more applications of it during the first year, but always very sparingly, rubbing off all that will come off on a soft cloth. When this is thoroughly dried it will polish beautifully with a soft silk cloth. It must never be applied hot or in any quantity, for it should not soak into the varnish but just remain on the surface. As previously stated. it is quite a mistake to imagine that Cremona varnish has just certain materials according to some formula; it contains, no doubt, all the materials in common use in Italy at the time, and different makers used different mixtures. It is the ratio of linseed oil used that accounts for the peculiar lustre and the velvety feel. This necessarily means a slow drying varnish. Do not make the mistake of former violin-makers who threw away Cremona varnish for quicker drying varnishes. It is the oil in the varnish that gives the lovely refinement of tone, and the elasticity and lustre in Cremona varnish. Now, I have said nothing about using hard, transparent wax for making varnish. I know this material is equal to the resins when used as foundation, and therefore it would be suitable material to go into varnish; but frankly I have never learned how to fuse it into varnish, though it seems reasonable that it could be done, and if so, one could find in it the consistency of varnishes made with resins. I have never felt the need for such varnish, and therefore have not taken time to go into it sufficiently to prove whether it could be made a success or not. As to using pure amber, I should think it would not be difficult to get the right proportions of amber and oil to yield the consistency that is best for Cremona tone. The amber varnish of commerce sold for violin varnish has not the exact lustre of the Cremona; and I believe that is because of the lack of oil in it. The man who thinks Cremona quality is confined to just one mixture and one recipe is mistaken.

The variety is infinite that will give Cremona quality."

⨤

Also got a nice note from the present owner of my first viola. He quoted appreciatively my modest label:
"My first, a hasty thing, Homely face, but loved to sing."

⨤

Also a letter from a retired person who is taking up violin making. ". . . I am a pretty good country fiddler and I enjoy repairing one once in a while." Read in a 1960 issue of the BC Journal about a violinist who switched to piano because the beer kept falling off his violin. Hope none of my readers is shocked by all this, all true.

⨤

I recall over the years working on some cheap fiddles with pressed backs, some of which had been obviously jointed after "bending/pressing". This was obvious from the joint on the inside, which had not been leveled. One finds all manner of "value engineered" dodges in the older factory fiddles. About a dozen variations from Jackson-Guldan alone. And of course the laminated instruments might also be considered "moule," in a different sense. Now used only on cellos and basses, this was used on some postwar German violins, some good sounding, as in all these vagaries; one can't generalize. I have been told that a reputable, late Portland violin maker made some moules (not plywood), as a labor saving technique. About the "stacks of pressed plates" - usually times these are routed, but I have seen some in "kits" that appeared to be pressed. (No, I never assembled a kit, please!). These inventive techniques are not limited to any nationality, but are found in French, German, Japanese, American, etc. One of the silliest is the use of plastic ears on Suzuki scrolls, to simplify the router work, I suppose.

⨤

I recall hearing "makers' forum" bass bar discussions at past VSA meetings that degenerated into animation and little else. . . . Bars should be "sprung;" certainly when replacing. (This rules out the integrally carved bars of some cheap Saxon stuff - a few of which, yes, sound good, too.) The optimum amount and distribution of spring varies. If a bar has to be replaced, it's not because it has worn out, but was not right when installed or was trimmed too much subsequently. A (correctly "tuned") thinner, higher, bar is generally better (livelier) than a thicker, lower one, since it will have the requisite stiffness with less mass. I use a conventional thickness where glued, but taper plane the sides for this.

1998

Since we're still close to the Bolander topic, here's an interesting quote from his booklet, Bow Making, A Thousand Bows and a Tribute. "Now I am going to make a statement that will not enhance good will from some. The statement is not mine, but I believe in it to the fullest extent - Not more than five percent of the so-called master makers' bow in existence today are genuine." Comments?

⨤

This seems like another of those ideas with a sound basis that might be over-generalized. It applies in particular if only one, say medium, string tension is used. On a short (string length) viola this will be floppy and ineffective; on a long one it will sound choked, whereas on a typical scale it will have both good tone and volume. (This is what makes one string an A, another a D, etc.) One string doesn't fit all violas. Notice in particular that the A on longer violas may sound like it is, and may actually be, in danger of breaking; try a lighter tension string. Of course the word tension here is not a good one, any more than gauge would be. What I mean is the assigned "grade" of the string, e.g. dolce or forte or mittel, etc.

⨤

. . . has voted for Boetel's peg soap, which has been around for eons, others, myself included, for Hill's peg compound, of comparable longevity, I guess. I found Boetel's troublesome when the wax let loose. All commercial stuff is mixed up with wax, graphite, pumice, real soap, chalk, etc. Supposedly the golden mean of sticky and slippery. What works depends on what condition the peg is in. Hill's is best all around, I think, and hope whoever is making it now will carry on. I suspect Fredrik's recipe

contains too much graphite for general use :-) For emergency use only on children's fiddles where the pegs don't fit, and where fine tuners are used anyway, the product called Peg Drops can be used to stop slipping without harm. Wipe off the excess. Don't know what's in it; maybe a solvent, rosin, and moderator. (I have even occasionally used a drop of this under the bridge feet on shiny _lacquered only_ school fiddles where the bridge slides all over.)

⨤

[Raymond White's analysis had shown pine resin and walnut oil as major constituents in varnish from Santo Seraphin (2), Pietro Zanetto, Giovanni Tononi, Andrea Guarneri, Francesco Gofriller, David Tecchler (Pine resin and linseed oil)]
I was interested in the appearance of walnut oil in these findings, without any way to judge their validity, of course. In January I published a 3rd ed. of my cello making book, which contained a varnish recipe. I am not a varnish expert, and have for the most part avoided making it. But I had lots of requests for a varnish recipe, and this is what I provided. I have quoted verbatim the information below, a little long - it occupies a whole page in the book. It seemed very apropos here, so I hope no one will mind, and this is the best place for me to find out whatever may be wrong with it.
© 1997-1998 Henry Strobel, INFORMATION ON VARNISHING as in his video Violin Making - Live! Varnish application: This will be clear from watching the video. It is basically the same as described in detail in Violin Making, Step by Step, pages 71-77, with the following differences, largely matters of choice:
- A yellow spirit varnish for the golden ground coat instead of yellow oi varnish.
- The main (color) varnish is made from the recipe below instead of the Hammerl Öllack or similar.
- I did not use a clear "overcoat" varnish.
Schedule of coats used in the video: (Smooth after each coat with a fine abrasive pad, if necessary.)
1. Water, followed by thinned (50/50) "salmon-color" (Hammerl/GEWA 464.004 Beize gelb) water stain.
2. A "sealer" of Behlen's violin (spirit) varnish, thinned 50/50 with denatured alcohol, colored with "golden yellow spirit coloring extract," and applied quickly and superficially as shown in the video. Don't let it soak in.
3. The "ground," another coat of the same, but not so thinly applied.
4. A coat of the "cooked oil varnish" described below, in its natural brown color.
5. Main (color) varnish 2 or 3 more coats of the same. The number of coats may vary with your formulation, color concentration, viscosity, and brushing technique. We want adequate color depth without excessive thickness; ideally the cooked varnish will have the desired hue and intensity of color already built-in, depending on your taste, cooking procedure, and amount of iron. (In this case, I also added some "brown oil coloring extract," Hammerl/GEWA 464.157. One has to "overcolor" with the extract; its color intensity lessens as it dries and will otherwise fade. See NOTES, Color: below.) First take the time to do full test sample schedules on a piece of wood, letting each coat dry thoroughly in the sun. Thin the varnish with a little pure spirits of turpentine if necessary for brushing. Follow the rubbing and polishing instructions in the video. A good violin varnish like this does not become hard or friable, remains very slightly plastic and self healing, but does not normally stick or print. Good prepared violin oil varnishes are readily available; do not cook your own unless you are skilled, and very careful! CAUTION - COOKING VARNISH IS EXTREMELY HAZARDOUS. I assume no responsibility for the suitability or safety of this information! The dangers of fire and toxic fumes require it to be done completely outside. Use a high-walled pot of about 10 times the volume of the cool material on an electric hotplate. Wear safety glasses. Don't breathe the fumes; use a suitable mask or ventilation system. Plan for emergencies.
NOTES
- At the beginning of the video I thanked my friend master luthier Robert Lundberg "for varnish making." He showed me how to make an excellent "Pine Resin & Walnut Oil" cooked varnish. I have adapted the method slightly as follows. It requires nothing

more complicated than an adjustable 750 watt hotplate, glass thermometer, porcelain-enameled pot, and a postal scale.
- Resin: "Pine resin" ("Harz" or "colophony") is used. Clear and light amber in color, this is essentially "rosin" without additives.
- Rationale: A number of past and present varnish makers begin by cooking the raw resins from the pine, fir, or larch (Venetian turpentine). This is also how bow rosin is produced, and "pure spirits of gum turpentine" is condensed from the volatile spirits of such cooking. Adding walnut or linseed oil to the remaining resin (rosin, in this case) and cooking further is a simple approach to varnish making, doubtless used for many early instruments. An evaporating thinner (pure spirits of gum turpentine again, or oil of lavender or rosemary, or naphtha, alone or combined) is added for brushability and leveling.
- Oil: Use edible cold-pressed walnut oil from the grocery.
- Color: Much of the brown color results from iron; I placed 10 antique 6-penny (50 mm) "cut" nails in 4 oz of resin. The use of an iron pot is an obvious alternative, and doubtless an historical one, but adding small pieces of iron (or even steel wool) gives better control. Even though the varnish looks very dark when wet it will lighten as it dries to a transparent, lightfast, golden brown, which may even darken over time, so don't overdo the iron. Omit the iron for an "uncolored" varnish. Or optionally glaze or add color from lake, earth, or suitable aniline colorants if wanted   with the usual difficulties that attend coloring oil varnish.
- Drying: A normal coat dries in a day, but sun is required. Metallic driers are not used, but some colorants have that side effect.
- Pure spirits of gum turpentine is the vehicle, or thinner, which evaporates away in drying.
TO MAKE "Pine Resin & Walnut Oil" VARNISH (See the sample weight record below.)
1.   Place the iron in the ceramic pot and weigh it. Add 100 to 150 g crushed resin (I used 4 oz or 114 g in this example) and cook 6 to 8 hours at 450°F (232°C), reducing the resin to a fraction of its original weight. Keep the thermometer bulb completely immersed in the hot resin for accuracy. Try to maintain the 450ø temperature, but there will be bubbling and frothing up and smoking initially and one or more exothermic temperature rises, but not drastic in my experience. When a light crust forms over the entire surface, and the pot has a medium smoke, the resin is ready for the oil.   (These are the instructions, but don't be surprised at variations, depending on the resin, apparatus and temperatures. The   smoke is temperature dependent and hard to interpret. One batch using Hammerl "Harz" crusted in 5 hours and stopped. Another experimental batch using raw resin from Indiana jack pines (pinus Banksiana) never did really crust, and   I stopped at 8 hours; there were also tiny bubbles that continued through part of step 2. Both made good varnish.)
2.   Remove the pot from the heat. Weigh it and subtract the weight of the pot and nails to get the weight of the remaining resin. Add walnut oil equal in weight to 2.5 times this. Place the pot back on the heat, raise the temperature to 500øF (260øC). There will be nasty fumes. Cook until the mixture passes the string test, in about 1 to 1.5 hrs. (A drop is placed on the back of a steel spoon to cool briefly; a fingertip should be able to touch it and draw a fine string about 2 in or 50 mm.
3.   Remove the pot from the heat and let cool to 125øF (52øC) or lower. Weigh again and subtract the weight of the pot and nails to get the weight of the new, unthinned, "varnish." Carefully add "pure spirits of gum turpentine" equal in weight to 2 times that of the combined resin and oil, less for a thicker varnish. Stir thoroughly. Remove the nails. Filter. Store in glass jars; it lasts for years.
Before heating:

Pot	8.8 oz
Pot and nails	9.8 oz
Added rosin	4 oz
After cooking rosin 5 hr at 450° F:	
Weighed pot and contents	11.5 oz
Less pot and nails	-9.8 oz
Reduced rosin =	1.7 oz
Added 2.5 x 1.7 oz oil =	4.25 oz
After cooking rosin&oil 1 hr at 500° F:	
Pot and contents	14.6 oz
Less pot and nails	-9.8 oz
Unthinned varnish =	4.8 oz
Added 2 x 4.8 oz spirits =	9.6 oz

Very good example of the confusion from common names. I have referred to Manilkara bidentata in the past as "beefwood" because of its appearance, similar I guess to "horseflesh," but neither of these names is used in the _bow_ trade where the term "brazilwood" is nearly universal. By the way, I will be removing the reference to beechwood in my article. It just occurred to me that it's been quite a few years since such a bow walked into my shop, although many years ago (as in my youth) they were not uncommon articles of German manufacture. Otto Moeckel in Die Kunst des Geigenbaues mentions it as used for the cheapest bows (fuer billigste Bogen verwendet). Most of these have been burnt by now. (On the other hand, we still have plenty of the wooden "coffin" cases coming in, and I usually extoll their merits in starting fires on cold mornings to the proud owners.)
The horseflesh - or Bulletrie wood, usually called Brazilwood (in English Beefwood or Bullet Tree, in French Buletrie), from Guyana supposedly from mangrove-tree, genus Rhizophora, which thrives in the low-lying sandy areas on the coasts of South America, the east and West Indies, as well as of Africa.

Plastic wood is OK, I would think, on the right violin, in a place where it isn't noticeable, to fill a small void, if it is reversible (removable), and where more cutting would be too costly or the greater evil. I knew an amateur maker who would simply plaster over with plastic wood when he gouged too deeply; we're not talking about this! I do remember rebarring a certain Pressenda. The front had been half-edged, but the upper and lower block areas had since lost lots of wood from tough openings. Someone had simply slathered on the plastic wood, lots of it, to fill these areas. I replaced this with wood, of course. (The owner subsequently sold this through a Chicago company for a very handsome price.) Using this stuff has an obvious advantage over joinery, in that no original wood is lost, the same rationale as I use in building up eroded ebony frogs with black cyanoacrylate instead of planing and gluing on a cheval of wood. . .

I think too that back removal is a very rare requirement. Separating the back button from the heel for work on the neck is much more common. Ben Ruth had a fine article in the VSA Journal just arrived on this. I recall about 10 years ago I reset the neck on an Enrico Rocca violin. This was at the request of the owner to correct a very low overstand. Apparently Rocca had written notes on the upper block. I decided to keep the shell of the upper block (and the handwriting), and essentially hollowed it out to fill with a new block in order to be able to do a good sound reset. (Yes, I did get an excellent match of the rays with the heel shim.) About the other item mentioned of using a small hammer to safely, gently, incrementally, propel the opening knife; that is something I do too. (Not at the initial insertion, of course, which could easily break a rib!) It is often almost necessary on cellos and basses and is much less likely to take a leap when a section lets go. It also allows you to concentrate better on watching the progress of the opening, lest a crack should begin.

I just had an old violin in recently that had holes in the exact center of each middle rib. These were, as I recall, about 1.5 mm in diameter. I did not fill them, but certainly wondered, not having seen this before. (Perhaps for some dubious acoustical reason.) It briefly brought to my mind the story of the turn of the century Scottish violin dealer David Laurie, who wrote of seeing customs inspectors in St. Petersburg drilling holes in the sides to inspect instruments for contraband. He suggested to these Philistines that it would be easier to remove the endpin and look in. I'm not sure this story makes sense, but he wrote it.

1999

. . .about the appearance of ebony bushings. A fiddle so fitted was in the shop yesterday, and the bushings looked really ugly, not just unusual. Like a makeshift for someone who had a box of fat old ebony pegs but no boxwood or good shaper at hand ;-). Just my impression. No offense intended to anyone who likes them.

❧

Read with interest your ruminations on sound post setting. Some of us do this several times a day (I for one) and we probably all do it the way we were taught or taught ourselves. We get adept at our own way, and it may be inefficient to change. Like learning a new language (not, I realize, proportionate to sound post setting) or changing from WordPerfect (in my case) to Word, if one is a writer. Years ago I had a violin in from a maker, I think in Spokane, Italian type name that I can't remember (I could look it up). Anyway I was annoyed to find that the sound post had the setter "mark" on the bass side, having been set through the bass hole. The danger here is that one may try to rotate it to "correct" it (I don't always use the mirror first - I know) and end up with the post all wrong or damage the front. A standard or universal method, a lingua franca of luthiers is desirable in this case. Do you have setter mark of another kind - like a pencil line? Anyway, I looked up this luthier at the time in Wenberg and found he was a Campbell alumnus. (By the way, Tom Wenberg, an Oregon (ex Minnesota) friend of mine, is now Thomas Wilde, a Democratic Oregon state senator here in Salem.) I asked Ed Campbell about this at the time and he spoke zealously of the benefits of setting through the bass hole. I was unconverted.

❧

Certainly the best way of mastering the underappreciated art of bow rehairing is to learn from a master, but for the rest of us there is a book available called Violin Maker's Notebook that would help in lieu of that and costs less than one rehairing fee. Some of the other popular books tell you to tie the hair with wire, which is not professional. No one becomes really expert at rehairing until the 100th bow, it has been said. (Perhaps some never do.) Best not to attempt a valuable bow until then. As for the time required, it varies a lot with how much extra work has to be done - cleaning, polishing, recutting mortises (on cheap bows), recutting plugs or repairing damage (especially if the previous rehairer was inept), springing, straightening, renewing wrapping, etc. But the _actual rehairing_ shouldn't take the experienced rehairer much more than 15 minutes, and the damp hair will then dry, shrinking to the correct length in a few hours on its own, depending on the humidity. If the violinist has his motor running, I suppose you could _cautiously_ use a hair drier, but heat is always a hazard to the hair.

❧

What a refreshing declaration of a real-world, worthwhile work, amid all the artistic esoterica of varnishology and woodology. The numbers here are compelling, and kids need good fiddles that don't present awful obstacles to learning by being practically unplayable, never mind sounding bad. It's good business and can also be a public service and a little philanthropic. I have spent more time than I care to admit making these things work for the kids - at least I can say that I'm good and fast, and that's essential here. This routine work is hardly satisfactory for an artist, but seeing the little fiddlers light up is. I too confess to having a "sideline" of several hundred "rent to own" instruments. . . . Once you get out the out of the bottom lines, the wretched older cheap Europeans, plastic-eared suzukis, and increasingly rare all-American Jackson-Guldan type residue, the better quality new imported instruments, even in the smaller sizes, can be excellent in tone, at least those from my current suppliers. Practically all are carved now, even the cellos - and really graduated! _Some_ of the thousand dollar (or less) violins have tone, workmanship, and materials that I suspect would embarrass a goodly number of those here by comparison. Some of my suppliers in China and the Czech Republic have seemingly found the repeatable recipe for tone. Now I know this matter of inexpensive imports is not a popular topic, at least in America, but one we all have to live with. Good for the kids, maybe not so good for individual makers and dealers. A major dealer I know recently remarked that it was almost impossible to move the old brown German violins, previously the market staple, but now mainly good for making into lamps. We hardly need mention the situation in bows, not one to gladden Mr. Glasser. But it's an ill wind that bodes nobody good. (I am speaking here of functionality for students, not personal preferences for artists. The antiquemongers will always do OK. I hope these remarks are not too inartistically commercial. I remain

an ardent lover of old violins. I do not mean to generalize, and I do mean to keep in mind the international character of this forum.)

❧

On rereading my last piece wherein I commented on some of the remarkably good trade violins we are now seeing, I thought perhaps I might have offended someone, and would like try again (I mean try not to offend!) It's always difficult to figure out the violin, to sort out its functional value vs. its artistic value as an object. We think of artistic violins as being unique, individual, perhaps asymmetrical, rare, antique, beautiful looking, sounding, working, with a bit of interesting provenance for good measure. Some of these features cost a lot relative to the musical functionality. Let's face it, the violin has been done before, and if we could clone a good one with good manufacturing quality control, these might be desirable as musical instruments ("student instruments") but would never be valuable art objects. Some, as Schleske, might try to do this precisely, individually. OK, so we can't really make two exactly alike (I sure can't and wouldn't), but what I am seeing are some "handmade" mass production facilities making remarkably good and uniform instruments, which all look alike and sound well and similar. This is akin to the earlier folk factories of Mirecourt, etc. that turned out quantities of precisely, uniformly, finished fiddles, but not executed by one integrating, individualizing artist. These people are the "professional violin makers," turning out two before breakfast, scraping cleaner and faster than most of us could, by dint of need and continuous, monotonous practice, without soul-searching or reinventing anything. Compared with some of them, some of us would be considered highly paid dabblers. But such is the desire for a unique and personal tool, costing a piece of my life and my care, that someone will pay me tenfold what he would pay for an anonymous clone of perhaps comparable functionality and likely tidier scraped. The violin is a lot of things to a lot of people. What it is to us, and what it means to be a violin maker are areas for comment perhaps. No offense, I trust.

❧

Scoop (or longitudinal concavity) of the fingerboard may be thought of in terms of the string height over the board at any point along its length. That doesn't help by itself, but it points up a number of related considerations: The string is harder to press down (stop) nearer its ends, so the string height should be less there. (especially for youngsters, Jean :-) The most common problem on new student violins is the outrageously high nut.) The greatest string displacement amplitude (not for every vibration, but for the greatest) will be in its center. (The mathematicians can correct me if this is wrong.) That doesn't mean the static string height should be very high in the center; the amount of scoop is often exaggerated. If the scoop is excessive, it has to be decreased by planing and in any case the string height at the ends must not be too high which compounds the difficulty of stopping. (Incidentally, here is meaning no. 15 from my Random House Dictionary for "stop."

> 15. a. to close (a fingerhole) in order to produce a particular note from a wind instrument.
>   b. to press down (a string of a violin, viola, etc.) in order to alter the pitch of the tone produced.
>   c. to produce (a particular note) by so doing.)

But a certain minimum string height at the ends (indeed everywhere) must be maintained to enable good vibrato and left hand pizzicato, and of course to prevent buzzing, which should go without saying. What I occasionally find on an older instrument is that someone has scraped away the furrows and pits from wear in the lower positions but was too lazy to remove the nut for proper planing, leaving an excessive string height only in the third or so near the nut, although not at the nut, and thus a "speed bump" farther down the fingerboard. The scoop must be smooth and gradual and never negative! This unfortunately is found frequently to plague young students whose fingerboard was never made right, or warped while the green wood seasoned, or while it was shipped with the strings tight down against the fingerboard, or was compressed in the packing case. (In marginal cases the position marking tapes teachers use can also cause buzzes.)

❧

(How might one tone down a shrill, bright sounding E string?) I doubt there's anything I can tell you that will be very helpful, especially since you asked specifically about bridge-cutting, which is not likely to be a silver bullet in this case. Hopefully someone out there more expert in this area will come forward. Usually this is part of a larger problem where the violin is just too thick, as on the basically ungraduated "student" instruments with a "wiry" or "brassy" sound. We see this kind of problem often on that caliber of cello too, where we first replace the "banjo" A string with a Larsen or Jargar, or at least put a rubber donut under it at the bridge to dampen it. Thinning the middle front will certainly affect the E string, but I have no idea of the quality or kind of instrument you are speaking of, or its thickness distribution, and probably regraduation is not an option for you. If it is actually some sort of special upper register resonance on a thin violin, disregard everything I have said. PS I assume you have tried a light gauge, wound E string?

&

While it is true that many new fingerboards, especially from emerging economies where they are trying to keep the machining of raw materials at home, may indeed be warped or have imprecise upper surfaces (lack of any scoop not being unusual on these), most of the high quality ones I have used from good suppliers are very close. I would rather correct this curved surface where needed than totally recreate it several mm down. While some may shudder, I find the easiest way to remove the excess bottom bulk is on a stationary belt sander. Yes, I know, the inept can quickly make a mess of this, rounding the surface and going too far, etc. But the "ept" should find that this abrasive milling technique is easy and fast. (We plane fingerboards all the time in the repair business, but I prefer not to do massive stock removal with my fingerboard plane.) The board is then placed on the neck and the sides marked for rough trimming by plane, allowing for a slight bit of flare (and flair). The fairing of the fingerboard edges into the neck is of course done (after lightly gluing it on) with file/plane & scraper. Small adjustments to edge thickness and scoop and are then made.

&

. . . "for what it may be worth," again, here is what I think about the old violin questions, unsubstantiated as is usual in the world of violins: That there are no significant undiscovered, widely and anciently applied, or essential, "secrets" for the apparent superiority of old master instruments. That these artistic and crafty geezers may have individually tried some magical things with their wood and varnish, as some still do, none of these was a requirement for, or of itself a reason for, excellence. A few may have salted or soaked or baked or stored their wood with the manure-whatever; these are not any general causes of excellence. (I am not addressing bending here, or the "Cremona varnish.") My customers are always asking why old violins sound better. "If they do," I say, it's because the bad old ones have been fixed or burnt. Well, it isn't that simple of course - there are still enough bad old ones around, and consider what we have just been discussing about various tone preferences, modernizing, etc. which in themselves make it hard for the acousticians to even define the problems. Consider the advantages of centuries of selection and finicky restoration and fame and rarity and wishful thinking and snake oil that goes with "investment" in antiques. (And, as Ivar says,"the fiddle doesn't play itself.") Consider too some of the "modern Italians" that brought big prices because of romantic associations and euphonious names - not because of their over-sturdy and indelicate carpentry. No, it isn't that simple, and I have adjusted and played so many good and bad, old and new, clunkers and zephyrs (and even made a few) to think that the differences in the wood are significant, in addition to the usual graduation and tuning methodology. (I note the recent comments here of Chladni practitioners indicating there is no sure-fire standard for plate tuning, and any one who perceptively works on lots of very good, but very different violins, must know this.) What I am thinking though is that some wood itself sounds better, perhaps has a frequency variant damping that sounds strong but not strident, and a diminished density that speaks fast and facilely. The varnish has a part in this, but it's superficial (no pun intended) and changing - it's mainly the wood, primary but very slowly changing, and some wood, indeed much old wood is different. More opaque and lighter, for example, two differences often noted, and these probably occurred gradually _after_ the

violin was made. Internal stress relief perhaps also. Playing-in may have something to do with it over a long time, although this term is more usually used to move a stubborn fiddle out of the shop until the player (hopefully) gets used to it. Well I think I'll go relieve some stress with a glass of red and pre-prandial cheese.

&

Karl Roy kindly decoded the faded label on the small viola I had mentioned below as; Johann Guellich (Guelich) Lauten und Instrumentenmacher in Mannheim Maerz 1799. Died 1837, son and successor to Mathias G. 1714-1803. Not one of the stellars.

&

(About painting the sound holes and pegbox inside) I forgot to mention that the burnt umber (not black!) from the tube is thinned quite a lot with spirits of turpentine. This also makes it dry faster, gives a more desirable matte finish, and of course doesn't build up too thick. Any that gets out of line is _easily_ wiped off the varnish with a paper towel. And everyone knows that burnt umber oil paint (undiluted) under the edges and perhaps in the corners of the scroll and mostly wiped out gives a mellowing understated effect - if desired.

&

This business of size names is a kind of language that violin people are born into and are probably stuck with. As English is the predominant language of commerce today, the "German" way of naming violin sizes is the most entrenched, whatever its systematic or not development. (It does not yet have a word for the baby bass.) There are Japanese and Italian (and even German) size dialects that we occasionally have to use or translate. Etymology is interesting, and logic attractive, but a consistent new system of sizing or naming is unlikely of adoption and would require more translation. My purpose in originally publishing the size tables in "Useful Measurements for Violin Makers" was simply to provide a dictionary of the language in use for those who, like myself at that time, were getting into the violin business and needing to know what was called what. Too bad we couldn't just designate them by the actual length in cm (or inches), as we usually do violas.

&

My books never pretended to be able show a novice how to predictably make a wonderful sounding violin in any context. Hundreds of years and this forum and the CAS can't do that. The books (and the schools) mostly show a workmanlike methodology. A good craftsman could make a pretty OK violin just after examining and measuring one without books or instruction - although he would probably do it inefficiently and overlook some conventional esthetic and chemical points. On the other hand, I have seen a number of violins made by amateurs with the help of my books, and there is, frankly, a very large range. (Of course they all sound like violins.) I have always strictly avoided saying that a particular graduation or tuning will in general result in a good sound. Hopeful, sensible, traditional, suggestions, is about it. If it is anything at all, good violin making is still an art, as good cooking is an art, even when we use the same recipes. The flavor of the apples will vary, among other things. As do tastes, both objective and subjective. Another term that sets me off is "student violin." A student violin is one that a student uses, and it may sound nasty or wonderful, be well made or horribly, but the student needs all the help he can get. Good adjustment is essential but good sound is next. Maybe a student violin is one that a professional would not like to list in his resume (for a variety of reasons, some non-technical), but many low priced violins are great sounding nowadays, and that's good.

&

It's been one of those days. I've was repairing the scroll on a wonderful viola today, broken in two when stepped on in a gambling establishment, I am told, but the owner had glued it with cyanoacrylate. Fortunately the solvent did not attack this particular varnish, but unfortunately neither could I get good hide glue to hold the denatured surfaces properly, complicating the reinforcement. Among other things.

&

I watched a friend making slightly "holey" wood into a violin, said it was good wood, with added character, and of course that is done in copying, whether with natural or contrived beetle holes. But the evidence is in favor of natural infestations occurring long after the instrument was built. We see damage so bad that no one could have intended it or even used such wood. You are right for instruments that are properly stored or frequently used, but over the years this is often not the case. Worm damage can occur in any improperly stored piece of wood. . . Just a couple of more observations on woodworm damage. It's relatively rare on modern instruments, more frequently evident on old ones, which have had many more occasions for exposure through cycles of war, insect plagues, improper storage, etc. Often the damage is old but has been poorly repaired. Restoring it can be daunting when substantial areas have been destroyed. I have some nice old instruments with only a few little holes and patches, and these can provide a feeling of age, charm and deserving survival, but I had in recently an otherwise good Gand violin that was so ravaged I declined to work on it. Some of these bugs seem to cut a wider swath than others. . .

         ❧

(On dichroism) Perhaps; I'm beginning to wonder if the whole thing isn't another instance of fiddle blather. Certainly some varnishes seem redder when thick and yellower when thin, and dichroic has been used to describe this. Dichromatic appears to generally simply mean two colors in various situations. Dichroic is used nowadays to describe mirrors, filters, polarizers, etc. that use a multiple thin film deposition technique. I guess something such _might_ occur fortuitously at complicated boundaries in a varnish job? Personally, I never saw a violin that provoked me to say," Wow, how dichroic!"

         ❧

Well, this is interesting, and one could warm up to this kind of inquiry. My first reaction was what does it matter what we call it - dichroism, fluorescence e.g., if we have a varnish system that exhibits the beauty we like -"warmth, fire," e.g. But of course the answer is that if we understand the mechanism(s) we might learn how to control it (them) or enhance the effect(s). Many of us know empirically how to do a pretty varnish, and not all the same way. For me it's a matter of beautiful wood selection, clean wood surface preparation, an appropriate gentle "pinkish pre-stain," grounding with a yellow clear varnish (fast drying, low penetration, and appropriate index of refraction - no hide glue please), and covered with a desirably complex "red-brown" varnish, probably containing small particulates/pigments. This may look prosaic, dull, or off-color in various artificial lights or in the shade, but take it into the energetic, collimated, broadband sunlight, which penetrates into the curly wood surface and it will "glow," for sure. This is more or less the level at which the typical artist violin maker works. But it brings us to the subjective, philosophical, physiological questions of what we are looking at, what we are looking for (a candy apple?), aren't we seeing selected light (as opposed to a violin), and should it be optimized for the light of 18th century or 21st century concert halls, or museum displays, or for playing in the park? And don't the best violins have their sparkle in their sound, rather than in their often vestigial varnish? But I digress.

2000

Sorry I sent a test message in error; please disregard. I seem to be making more than my share of mistakes this week. Sunday was a bright spot, however. Went to a concert in Salem, heard a world premier of a Scottish suite for cellos by a local composer. Two of the cellos were mine, and the humble maker was introduced from the back wall of the SRO audience. That's really what this stuff is all about.

         ❧

Interesting and useful report. This is what many might call, in other words, a wolf correction. Violins generally do not have warbling wolves, as cellos, but often a wild or unpleasant note(s) in the lower A string, analogous to the wolf. Often improved by moving the post closer to the bridge, but as you indicate, more extreme in your case. I suspect not completely assignable to Mr. Fry, however.
(What is a golf correction? Oh, you said "wolf". Oops.) I don't know - and probably never needed one, although I know some board members who probably do. (Some of us may have needed a wolf correction in younger days.) I never actually golfed, although I made a symbolic circuit of Old Troon while on active

duty in Ayrshire. I do have at hand here "The Golf Omnibus," Thirty-One Humorous tales from the Green by P.G. Wodehouse, which I read more for the author than the subject. Perhaps I could look it up -

         ❧

Nippon (prewar) violins have elicited some interesting comments. It is fair I think to observe this is only an indication of period and national origin and there are probably variations (why not?). The several I have sold have the Nippon label inside the right soundhole, good carving (apparently not pressed or bent), well graduated with tone to match, little flame in the wood but a good brown varnish. I have seen a _neck_ or two of some interesting wood that looks like a "blond pernambuco." The Nippon brand on bows particularly is accompanied by a sort of double cloverleaf device, and the frogs are usually of a rather porous ebony, often a lacquered stick.

         ❧

The first time I tried dedamping a violin (before I published the book, and one of the reasons I did), I also observed an improvement (previously reported, but only subjectively measured). This was on a personal violin I had made 17 years ago and not played much. It had always been even but (apparently) never so loud or responsive or pleasant. This was strongly vibrated with a motor assembly provided by Prof. v. Reumont, and I had difficulty in keeping the bridge position stable (leaving its mark on the varnish). My violinist son was quite impressed with the improvement.

         ❧

It was at the very end of 1999 that I opened this topic here in an exploratory way. As the discussion resumes perhaps I can make some general observations. My initial impression was the typical one of skepticism - followed by fascination. Lothar Tews has recounted the background, the book, his translation, and my publishing of it in English. It is a seductive subject, and like many things in violin making, not that easy to tie down scientifically. But as you know from my recent posts - I have used it and it is real as far as I am concerned. But as the discussion shows there are unclear areas and objections, some technical, others traditional. Questions abound about the limits and parameters, and most of all - how it is objectively measured. The book is both a how-to (as announced in its title) and a history of the author's experience and findings. I think it is an important one in the art of violin making. As I have noted in disclaimers in the book and on my web site, I am the publisher, not the author or an expert in this area, also that vibration dedamping as presented is more of an art than a science, and
the author, whom I know and respect, would be the first to agree. Yes, there are probably errors in the current data and its interpretation. But that doesn't mean that the process doesn't work, or that the observations and advice are not correct and useful! I was greatly encouraged by Dr. Gottfried Lehmann's further research in this area, having received a preliminary copy of the paper which is hopefully soon to be published. Sadly, he is ill, casting uncertainty on the date. Given the incentives of the benefits of this process, I feel sure that the blanks will be filled in, and that certainly there are those in this forum who could be instrumental in that, or who will at least make practical use of the procedures. Under the circumstances, I feel I should say that, yes, the test results show objectively measured changes (before and after differences) that plausibly correlate with the subjectively observed improvements. The changes include an increase in level and, probably more importantly, in the number of resonance peaks.

         ❧

I would agree. I have numerous times lowered a bridge because the strings were too high and found that the fiddle played more easily (well of course it wood) and sounded richer. Some of this might of course be simply removal of muting mass at the top, but probably also from a kind of "stress lessening"

         ❧

Someone recently showed me an old videotape of an SCAVM symposium of several years ago in which Bruce Harvie spoke about tonewood. If I recall correctly he seemed to say that Western maple (acer macrophyllum) is often tan in color, but that this is usually a result of the harvesting process and is the result of fungus more than the natural wood color, and that the whiteness of European maple is maintained by the skill of those who cut it (in the winter when the sap is low) and carefully season it. In more advanced cases the fungus also makes the wood a little "punky" and difficult to carve cleanly, which I have noticed in some otherwise great tonewood. (Remember Dr. Nagyvary's fungus theory?) I just spoke with Bruce on the phone, and he said this was basically true - also that he had just contacted Claire about joining, so perhaps this is a little premature - but I thought it might be an interesting thing to talk about. In the early days here back in 1995 and subsequently there were many good wood discussions, which the newer members will have missed. I doubt that the veterans will want to relive these in detail, and not likely the pernambuco saga, but perhaps in summary, or perhaps with newer insights.

I too filter varnish sometimes. I use cloth followed by wine makers' filters. They remove the bits of bark and bugs from the resin picked off pine trees ;-) . . .The filters I have look like ordinary circular lab filters (and perhaps are?) but are boxed as "Green's 940A Filter Paper for wine making, 240 mm diameter, Extra fast filtering, Leigh-Williams & Sons, Tottenhall, Nr. Chester." You can probably get the equivalent at any local wine making supplier. (I used my cabernet sauvignons in the back yard a time or two-)

Reflecting on the lackadaisical condition (here), I was reminded of a wonderful book by journalist/humorist H. Allen Smith called Lost in the Horse Latitudes. (This mail would generally be characterized as a "test.") Except that the August Strad just arrived bearing a good brief review of the von Reumont book by Joseph Curtin. (Thanks, Joe, if you read this.) I hope to have something new to report soon in this area of vibration dedamping. I appreciate this quieter summertime shopwise, and Oregon seems to be one of the few places with the right weather.

Yes, I would hope we learn and improve as we go. It is a poor and unsuccessful artisan/artist who does not. Lots of experience, motivation, competition, quality control, feedback and education should result in a superior product. Technical excellence in the violin world is sometimes mixed with mysticism and romanticism, prejudice, conflict of interest (there's a biggie), and all the other subjective considerations. If we had several functionally excellent perfectly symmetrical violins, indistinguishable except that one was a bit "crooked," would that be the artistic one? In the current state of highly perfected, highly standardized "contest ideal" production, it would seem that "imperfections" are the only thing setting one instrument artistically apart. And yet paradoxically if one attempts to add individuality in the form of a Magginiesque purfling, for example, it is likely to be excluded as gauche. The visual aspects of a violin as sculpture or painting are not definitely linked to it's functional ones of tone and playability. The student seeking a good musical instrument, unencumbered by subjective bias is today in the best position ever. Some of the relatively affordable master instruments coming from practical, non prima donna, expert makers, in China for example, are as good (practically) as many others at (practically) any price, if we exclude history, show-biz, collectibility, etc. If you don't agree, you haven't seen and heard the ones I have. These makers have paid attention to the factors I mentioned at the beginning. These remarks are meant as sententious, not contentious.

I would like to ask, since you did not distinguish here, if the same figure of merit applies to maple as to spruce. Does this not depend on how the radiation is occurring? I somehow have the impression that the maple is often too stiff, and that a curly, therefore more flexible, back and ribs give, for example, a bigger, more responsive sound in cellos? (This might only be offsetting another problem. But this wood should be very low density also.) Such "figures of merit" are attractive and especially useful in that they are "aperiodic," as opposed to the quirks of plate "tuning." Another such might be the (frequency dependent?) damping characteristics of wood or structure dependent on age or, as you say, "treatment," perhaps even different in Venice or Cremona ;-), or following playing-in or "vibration-dedamping?"

(To a question re "aperiodic" above, whether similar to the phenomenon noticed that If removing a small shaving in a sensitive area, the shoulders of the bass bar, for example, causes an improvement, a second such shaving will invariably cause a reversion toward the previous state, while a third shaving may bring back the improvement in a slightly different manner as if the periodicity occurs on a spiral rather than a circle.) Not exactly what I was thinking about, but an interesting point. I saw an article reporting this years ago in one of the newsletters. I doubt it would work "invariably," however! But I do remember a session with a good customer many years ago. He was a violinist in a major symphony and also a private dealer, of whose fine instruments I was the caretaker. He talked me into, under some duress, surgically trimming a bar (in very small decrements) through the sound hole while he assessed progress stepwise. I am sure he actually heard and evaluated the changes, but I was non-plussed. My thought on an "aperiodic" characteristic would be one, as of, say "tonewood" that was desirable in instruments irrespective of size, model, etc., as the figure of merit we mentioned seems to apply, at least in a simple, more or less obvious and general way to spruce soundboards. On the other hand particular plate mode frequencies would be optimum for a particular size, model, and other specific context.

1.) It is the nature of this forum to discuss the pros and cons of various new things which we might or might not ever put into practice.
2.) We are perfectly free to try these things in our own instrument production, and this is how progress, if any, occurs, even though they might distress some future repairman.
3.) We ought never do things, however well-intentioned, which are outside the currently accepted conservative practices of the art to the property of others, whether of individuals or of what might be termed the public patrimony in the case of historically important instruments. Such things might be considered as reckless, illegal, or vandalism.

Many know the tinkerer who "improves" or "restores" violins by widening the sound holes to "let the tone out" or stripping the original varnish to "restore" them. It seems every area has one. There are too many dismal possibilities here to imagine. This may be a harmless hobby, assuming his violins are junk (if not they soon will be), but the danger is that someone else may pay to have his violin damaged, or even get it done for free. You are addressing, I think, a more difficult area, where professionals or intelligent amateurs may do things they think are beneficial but that may turn out eventually otherwise, or that may be considered erroneous or unethical by others. This has been going on for hundreds of years and has been part of the evolution of the violin under the lead of luminaries as Vuillaume. During the earlier years here there were warm and extended discussions of regraduation, etc. - those difficult areas where craft and conservatism and commercialism meet. Another "dilemma" in the world of the violin where things are not always what they seem?

Anyway, my translation was a bit flip, and I wouldn't be surprised if by now someone has suggested a more mundane/literal one, as ending "Now I sweetly sing." I wrote:
The life I lived in the forest, Was ended by a sharp-edged axe.
Oh, yes, I lived a quiet life, But now I sing to the max.
(translating the Latin:)
Viva fui in sylvis, Sum dura occisa securi,
Dum vixi tacui, Mortua dulce cano.

As long as we're trying to sort out rosin, perhaps someone can clarify the difference between "light" and "dark." We seem to use these terms as though they meant something definite or specific, regardless of mfg. Do they? Can some one enlighten as to what these terms mean to the performer - is it a matter (like turkey) of color or taste or "crunch?" or performance? And what do they mean to the rosin maker - cooking time, (green)food coloring or whatever? One sometimes thinks of the darker as being for some reason less dusty and stickier. There are summer and winter grades, varying in softening temperature? Some is prone to cracking when shipped at low temperatures, and some (as Pops) cannot be shipped in the summer because of excessive flow. Rosin too seems to be one of those violin areas fraught with folklore and marketing bologna. It has been sold containing all manner of metal filings, if not vitamin E.

᠀

(To a suggestion that my interests in violin related information were not historical but strictly utilitarian.)
Good grief, no. That would be quite a leap - from my finding little of varnishing use (to me) in a particular book about resins and gums (much of which I knew already). I did allow that others who are actively pursuing historical varnish information might "read between the lines" and perhaps find clues there. I reckon any artistic violin maker (I hope that includes me) is interested in varnish way beyond mere utility. I am in fact a collector of and burrower in old books (of many disciplines) and even have a modest collection of old fiddles. I'll bet that most of the classical violin makers troubled their heads much less than we do about varnish, probably picking it up at the Cremona hardware store. Lacking this source, I now use pine resin - walnut oil with iron. Mr. Fulton tells me this acid stuff will self- destruct and Mr. Darnton tells me this might be a good thing. And others say many other things. Ars longa and longa, vita brevis. So I have limited my answer to the varnish question, but similar considerations apply to "violin related information" in general.

᠀

I have in my hand here two bottles of oil varnish, gifts of Nevada violin maker Craig Dill. One is labelled "Light Yellow- Gold, Balsam (Canada) and Pine Rosin (sic)." The other is labelled "Dark Red Brown, Douglas Fir and Larch Turpentine." So apparently Douglas fir is usable. In fact it seems practically any of such resins can be used in making good varnishes. I have varnish I made from Jack Pine (pinus Banksiana) picked off trees in a golf course in Indiana.

᠀

You didn't specify what the back was on, but it reminds me of a pricey French cello played by a local artist. It has only a slight regular flame, but this is cleverly accentuated by superimposed brushed-on bands of color, a hybrid effect, and less obvious than the very common dead airbrushed "figure" seen on cheap student instruments, typically from Hungary. These latter can be ugly in the extreme, and hardly an improvement on the dead plain wood. Don't know why they bother.

᠀

I have seen lots of these bows, many more than real snakewood. You must have an unusual one, since most of the ones I see were anything but painstakingly done - more as if the fin-de-siecle equivalent of the magic marker was used. These often come with the odd curlycue "ivory" frog and are typically wimpy "brazilwood" sticks.

᠀

Remembering some of the references you have cited in the past from old publications, I was again reminded how the same topics keep recurring in the discussions of violin makers. A book dealer, aware that I might be vulnerable to offloading some of my collected violin trivia, asked if I had any copies of the British Columbia Violin Makers Journal. I found sixteen copies from the early sixties and began turning pages. This was from the time of the beginning of the Catgut generation, F. A. Saunders arguing with Kristian Skou about basic acoustics and of course "microtones," Michaelman's varnish, lots of correspondence from Clifford Hoing, Carmen White, Pasqualini, and Clarence Cooper's geometry. I decided to copy a few articles before passing them on. The BC Journal was at that barren time an international focal point for articles, correspondence and ads from all over. Some very good, some . . . Here is an ad from Feb. 61.

VIOLIN MAKERS - SOMETHING NEW - FOSSIL WOOD
Allow yourself the pleasure of owning an. instrument: with power, refinement and. nobility of tone. Try our Patent Fossil Wood, prepared by us from the finest European Spruce and German Maple. Write us and find out all about it. We supply wood for a complete instrument and at a moderate price. Fossil wood eventually becomes as hard as bone producing perfect tone. Write for particulars. Jan Hilbert Nordlander Gunnilse, Sweden

A good summary of grounds by Don White (editor for many years and a very nice man) in the Nov. 60 issue. I copied this as well as an article in the Nov-Dec 62 issue, which described two different items. One of these (somewhat Fultonesque) was a front with the middle section (that roughly between the sound holes) being bent to the "exact arch required, vibrations run rapidly from the bridge to both ends." This idea he got from "What Makes a Good Violin" by Arthur T. Walker, Pageant Press NY "A book every maker should own." (I never heard of it.) The other was the longitudinal brace running from upper to lower end blocks of 1/4 in square Sitka spruce, just low enough to clear the top plate. (I have actually seen a couple of these, nor were they new in Mr. White's time. The following excerpt I translated from L. Greilsamer's "Health of the Violin . . ." will serve.) "At the Exposition of 1867, M. Miremont exhibited a violin fitted with a second bar. M. Gallay accounts for the innovation in the terms: "We reserve our appraisal of the interior modification for which, we have been told, M. Miremont has received a patent. We were told of a second bar. If it's a matter of a second bar going from the upper block to the lower, it would be reminiscent of a system already conceived and proposed to the Gand brothers about fifteen years ago by an American luthier. "Before adopting this system and wishing to learn the effects of this peculiar fixture, the Gands agreed to set up some violins in this fashion, but the results were in no way conclusive. "The inventor especially wished to avoid the movement of the fingerboard projection that occurs sometimes on certain instruments, when, as a result of the pull of the tailpiece, the neck is pulled forward thus lowering the fingerboard; moreover, this supplementary bar would have the advantage of better sound distribution and prevention of bad notes."
M. Mordret, who was unaware of the work of M. Gallay had, in 1865, done similar experiments on his own, which he expressed thus:
"The fixture consists in a rod of spruce traversing the inside of the box and mortised into the ends of the two blocks; we have calculated the shape and dimensions for resistance to bending, the same over its whole length. "From the viewpoint of solidity, the result was what it should be, but from the viewpoint of sound, we were wrong in our expectation. The timbre and power did not change noticeably; but some notes, particularly among those on the fourth string, exhibited pulsating vibrations, whose effect was quite disagreeable. [We call these "wolf tones."] This phenomenon is explained thus: it results from too great a mobility in the sound board, having become isolated as a result of the rigid connection of the neck with the tailpiece. It produces these gratuitous jumps or nuisance effects, which was thoroughly understood by M. Savart when he said that the vibration of the box ought never take control of that of the strings. "And so, little encouraged by the result, we abandoned our experiments."
In this pre-Hutchins-Scientific American era Scandinavian Kristian Skou's microtone/microtuning system discussion went on through numerous issues. Somewhat similar to the Fuhr glass tube vibrating method and Vigdorchik's later zone tapping system, he would tap lightly on the violin while damping other areas with his fingers and make sure the "microtone" was same, front and back, in the same place. Skou also made this interesting comment about the difference in the molecular chains of the microfibrils of old and new wood shown by x-ray diffraction, that they are broken into shorter chains in old wood. (He collaborated with a scientist on this.) Well, enough of this meandering. I just thought some of the older gentlemen here might enjoy recalling such stuff.

2001

Happy New Year, Friends,
It has now been my privilege to be a member of this group for over five years. Apparently there are other fiddle forums out there - I couldn't say. But I'm sure from internal evidence that this is the best! Thanks to those who have founded and fostered it through the years. Like most families it has had its disagreements, which it has survived, thriving with good humor and a continuing membership of the best violin makers discussing the best information in our field, sharing it generously with each other and the juniors among us. The vast majority of our members, reticent or not, are still with us, a tribute to the value of what is said here,

and of the network it provides.

≈

Good comments on the pricing issue. While many might like reference schedules to help in setting their prices, these are things are really that have to be individually decided based on your market and business and what and how you repair. I could not and did not refer to any specific prices other than a $37.50 example for rehairing. This will be on the low side for quality bows, and a little on the high side for those offering bulk work for schools. (Sadly, in the case of some rehairing the customer should be doing the charging ;-) The $14,000 repair cited is from another world than mine, so I won't comment. But when I fit a bridge for someone in the Oregon Symphony it appropriately and necessarily costs a lot more than the one I replace on a half size rental. You mentioned time. True, time, as I said, is not of interest per se to the customer - to him it's the quality, cost, and promptness of the work that matter. To the proprietor, however, time is definitely a cost factor of interest, especially when he has a number of repair personnel and needs to set shop standards. Michael is no doubt familiar with the repair procedures and standard times worked up by William Webster in Chicago, for instance, years ago.

≈

I have no interest in entering the unending and unsatisfactory general discussion of science, art, tradition, etc. in lutherie. But here are some notes on a particular case, with which many of you will be somewhat familiar from past posts.
As you probably know I published a book on "vibration dedamping" (mechanical 'playing-in') translated by Lothar Tews, that had been previously published in German. It was written by Prof. Gerhard A von Reumont describing his extensive experience and success in this and how to do it in practice. I was impressed both by the book and by my own experience in applying it. My discussion of this was, you will recall, reserved and cautious, not only because I am this way by nature, but I had been crisply criticised for publishing it by two long-time friends of mine, one a foremost authority in traditional violin making, the other a foremost authority in "scientific" violin acoustics. The traditional objection was not unexpected, and the other was based partly on an error in measurement interpretation (which I have addressed), but more because he had never observed this effect in his measurements, and thus doubted its existence.
As you will also recall, further research in this area was done by Dr. Gottfried Lehmann, and Part I of this work was published recently in Instrumentenbau-Zeitschrift (the German magazine "Instrument Building"). Part II of his paper has now also appeared in the Nov-Dec issue. Both Lothar and I have been in touch with the Lehmanns over the past year, had early translated their paper, and expect they will soon publish it in English (where as yet unannounced).
This paper is recommended to you as providing the best yet objective observations and explanations of the effects of such playing-in. The Lehmanns, father and son, were assisted in their measurements to some extent by Martin Schleske. The most significant data presented seems to be in the increased numbers of coupled resonances measured, which is interpreted as providing increased modulabilty, etc.

≈

Just from your description of the dark coloring in the low areas, it sounds almost exactly (except for the _black_) like lots of old and not so old instruments look, a conventional stylized appearance. I don't think it comes from a dirty polishing cloth. Many applications of that give an overall dingy look, but it's not the same. (I do recall the remark by Charles Beare in the VSA article.) It's usually from a sort of glaze, let dry somewhat and wiped off the high areas, giving the dings a little class, sort of a reverse retouch. I think we'd be amazed at how many instruments, good ones too, have been subjected to such treatment. I saw a "Francesco Stradivari" cello being so "reconditioned" in a classy shop, with burnt umber in this case. You can see it in lots of pictures too. "Absolutely jet black" as you describe it is unexpected, although it is of course found in cheesier "antiquing." Another thing that (rarely) happens is that the varnish turns black and the instrument is lightened by stiff rubbing overall, but this is probably not the case here. Incidentally it occurs to me (as an unrelated matter of personal

taste) that I really dislike a cold black such as is sometimes seen in pegboxes, sound hole edges, or even the "classic" detailing of chamfers and rib ends.

≈

Several recently have well expressed points (no pun intended) on the use of steel or wood guide pins to glue fingerboards on. It seems perhaps this is a fix for a problem which should rather be dealt with directly, i.e a deficiency in gluing technique. Someone who glues fingerboards on everyday will not require crutches like this, and would not bother. Much of the work of the violin maker is not art or innovation but skill in such repetitive tasks, as using the fingertips as sensitive "feeler gauges" of alignment, the right glue, consistency, amount, temperature, clamping, etc. - born of experience. What seems like a good idea may have downsides as well. Blind (invisible) pins (especially steel ones) can be troublesome. Fingerboards do have to be occasionally removed, e.g to replace when worn or to repair a broken neck heel, etc., and the shock when the opening knife hits a steel pin is unpleasant. For the same reason fingerboards should not be glued on too strongly, and with the correct glue. (By the way I seem to recall studies have shown that scoring the underside of the fingerboard, as is frequently seen, does not contribute to a stronger joint. Whether it helps in some other way I cannot say.) Incidentally, a quick search of past postings turned up this tidbit - >. . . I have a request for information on violin maker Sergio Peresson: "his ideas, weights, etc." Can anyone help?
>>I presume you have a specific reason for this question; not much to go on. He is one of those modern makers who became >>hugely successful for several reasons, one being his relationship to the Philadelphia orchestra. New Jersey, born in Venezuela >>in 1913, see Wenberg's encyclopedia (cites fine workmanship but "many precarved parts" in later period i.e. '70s). Also a long >>nicely illustrated article in The Way They Play, Book 9 - if you can put up with the obsequious style of these books. I worked on a >>couple of nice Peresson violins 5 -6 years ago. The only things I seem to recall were the distinctively "squarish" upper f-hole >>wings (nice), and a fingerboard that was surprisingly glued on _very_ tight with metal alignment pins to boot.
Well, of course I can't be sure that he put those pins in or glued that fingerboard on. Concern for others who may have to repair an instrument in its centuries-long lifetime is also one of the reasons for always using the right glue with its predictable characteristics and known solvency. It is the reason for certain other conventions, such as setting the post from the right sound hole with the setter leaving a pierce mark in the right upper part. Setting (and marking) it from the left hole might lead to its being later rotated 180 degrees by someone who does not inspect it carefully enough. (This is not to counter Sam C.'s recently and nicely described alternative techniques. Indeed we often have to use workarounds in the case of too narrow soundholes or the very tiny instruments, but in most cases the conventional method is convenient and preferable.)

≈

Thanks for the fascinating local report. I do recall as a schoolboy seeing these violins in the Montgomery Ward catalog. They have frequently come through the shop for repair. The most common style I recall (there were several) is the simple linerless and corner blockless one. Also an odd neck block. Low fingerboards are endemic on student instruments, but usually more related to construction details and joint creep than wood. Yes, it would be interesting to know how they carved the homely scrolls - the tool marks indicate quite a different machine than the router type used on most European school fiddles. On another point, I can't recall if some of the bent or pressed plate boxes with the center inside join left uneven were Jackson Guldan or Thibouville , etc.

≈

I will have to go with Peter on this one, John. People are usually dichotomous in this area. When I lived in Ayrshire in the 60s I tested various brands - Glenfiddich, Glenlivet, Haig's Pinch, etc. Now at 65 I drink Oregon Pinot Noir with dinner and am more likely to build a ship model in the Pinch bottle than imbibe.

≈

Different strokes for different shops . . . etc. _but_ I don't trust _screws_ at all. They always come loose, at least the ones I've seen. (I guess I see them because they came loose ;-). The expansion coefficient is different, and the threads compress the wood, which gives and gives. No epoxy, true, but no Titebond either, as far as I'm concerned. A good maple dowel is usually the thing to do, although I know some shops have used a large spline in a saw cut, visible on economy jobs - I would not. Let me know what I'm missing here.

You make some good points, but I think it would be better to reinforce the neck join - at least in principle. That's not why I'm writing though; I was struck by the similarity with another car crash problem, the repair of which I described in detail in an appendix to my Violin Maker's Notebook. The neck of a good violin was broken right in half. I glued it, then routed out most of the inside of the neck with a cove bit and inlaid - you guessed it - a semicircular maple dowel, with the grain running (incontestably) the right way. Analogous to a sound post patch, in that you preserve the outside but replace the (broken) inside.

Many will be weary of this pinning topic, but private mail indicates further interest from some, so I thought I would take one more whack at clarifying it. (It is a basic thing that all repair shops have to handle, and many of you are more expert that this than I. Comments are welcome - I might be wrong about some of this!) The important thing is to understand the stresses in the joint, that it is under compression at the block side, but under tension at the outside, which tends to open the joint. Here is where the pin or spline needs to be. (A thick cross-grain spline set into a dado cut at the "crotch" is an effective alternative to the pin, but is more difficult, requiring a jig, and very visible, which may or may not be a good thing.) I was also asked why a reinforcement was even needed, since the glue was "stronger than the wood." A transverse neck heel glue joint, even a good one (or the unbroken wood itself) is not stronger than a properly placed dowel in tension. Also the outside of the dowel provides more (shear) glue surface, which helps to offset the cyclic weakening of the glue from environmental factors.

Well good, perhaps we are out of the doldrums. Makes a change from tinfoil vendors, albeit a bit grumpy sounding ;-) (I would have thought Strads were more ready to hand in the old country than rural Oregon.) Indeed I too felt that the article was not worth much, but merely brought it up for interesting comment by experts. You did not define "violin improving process," although you seemed to include design changes as well as external influences. Perhaps you were focusing on the latter? You are right - I cannot think of any that have not been around for very long. Two of the predominant such are:
1. The verbal improvement process, as practiced by dealers and as found in puff-art pieces in the Strad.
2. Playing-in, as practiced by definition.

I suppose I will be quoted from now on for this rather unfortunate comment, flip and tongue in cheek on a Monday morning. I would like to apologize straightaway to the Strad and any one else that it may have offended. We are constantly drawn in different ways in this business. On the one hand we are fascinated by the old instruments and their history and any new discoveries about them and our art. We are in this business because we like violins. We appreciate the work and patience of those who dig this stuff up. Along with this we sometimes wonder if some of the incentive, particularly in their eulogies of what might be, in a different context, mediocre work, is to add to the otherwise diminishing pool of profitable antiques. I do look forward to the beautiful illustrations and information that comes with almost every Strad.

Yes I think I remember, but not so well as I used to. Let's try here first. Most violins have a tendency to an unevenness or kind of a "lame" sound around c or so on the A string and at corresponding notes high on the g string, and this is usually when the post is too loose or too far from the bridge. Moving the post closer to the bridge often helps even this out. The distance of the post from the bridge is usually best when it is about equal to the thickness of the top in that area, typically about 2.8-3 mm. Less for a too thin top, more for a thick "music store" one. Wolfs also occur when the

front or the bass bar is not stiff enough. If you have a false deep sound (tubby) definitely try a higher bar. This is from my extensive repair experience - there are no particular wolf tendencies associated with the Bisiach pattern as such.

I have met only a few of you in person, but nevertheless feel I know many of you personally through our correspondence here and otherwise. We share a common interest, although from possibly differing perspectives. The violin is a personal instrument - we know what we like - and we pursue it diligently whether as performers or craftsmen, science or "expertise" not necessarily withstanding. The recent discussions have been interesting, bearing on the relevancy of tradition, craft, art, science, even philosophy and religion. These latter are not usually considered relevant for this forum, but they are very essentially relevant to the good life, individual and common. I have been quiet here on these matters, but have written on them, among other things, in a very personal way in a little book called "Reflections, Personal Essays," which some in fact think is well and entertainingly written. No, this is not an advertisement, but an invitation to those friends here who might like a copy as a gift. I have a small number of fine hardbound "printer overrun" copies outside the limited edition of 500; if you would like one, write me, preferably including postage. It is introduced and excerpted on my website, so you can see there whether you are interested.

P.S. Now a sad bit of news. Dr. Gottfried Lehmann passed away recently. He was however thankfully able to see his landmark paper on vibration dedamping published in the German periodical Instrumentenbau Zeitschrift.
Kind regards and Merry Christmas to all,

2002

This will not be of interest to many, so I will be brief. Most of us simply and practically use whatever browser, etc. they find installed on the computer. But my perspective is different for three reasons:
1 - being a former electronic engineer I try to configure mine as simply and efficiently as possible.
2 - being a writer and publisher as well as proprietor of a violin shop, we use computer(s) daily as production tools, and everything on them is no nonsense, no frills, solid as possible over years, and with bulletproof backups.
3 - I like to choose my applications and not have them forced on me by a monopoly.
I use a fast, reduced version of Windows, with no Internet Explorer, no games, no video/dvd players, no clipart, no MS publisher or Front Page or Office, etc. (I do have a few .mp3s ranging from Fritz Kreisler to Emmylou Harris ;-) The applications I use is another story, but you asked about Opera. Opera is from Norway, and is the only real alternative to IE and Netscape. It is small, fast, convenient and very flexible, once you know how to optimally use and configure it (of course). It has good indicators so you know what is going on. You can very simply control and turn on/off cookies, pop-ups, javascript, etc. (I would not use its email client - as I would not use Outlook Express - Eudora is much better.) Opera is very popular in Europe, is available for 5 operating systems, and is very standards compliant. I have used it for about 5 years, and yes it's much better than it used to be. But admittedly this choice is largely a matter of personal preference.

I commiserate, having known a few varnish setbacks too. I do want to note though, that it is hard to generalize reliably about the results of "spirit varnish" over "oil," etc. To illustrate this I have attached a .jpg photo of a violin I made in 1982 (20 yrs ago). I cannot recall the specific brands or formulations, but I definitely recall that this was a case of spirit varnish (colored with Bismarck brown) over oil varnish (colored with some aniline yellow) over a spirit varnish ground, all applied within days. The crackle matured in a few months, and remains unchanged, all the varnish perfectly sound. (The white look of the crackle and the milky cast is due to the way I used the sun to show up the crackle for the backyard snapshot this afternoon. It does not normally look white at all.) I have not varnished this way for quite a while, but I see nothing wrong with a little stable crackle. Sorry if the photo slows down your email.

(Editorial note - You can see this photo in great color and detail at www.HenryStrobel.com/crackle.jpg, along with many others.

Hello, time to close shop for the day, unfortunately not for the week, "Tubes." - I'm referring not to the containers that gut strings come in, but the multipurpose tubular items that the string slides through over the bridge. These are normally, as I understand it, intended for string protection, tone control, and bridge protection (from the "cheese cutter" action of high pressure steel strings). I have set up several thousands of violins, but it is only fairly recently I have been using some of the inexpensive Prelude strings as supplied with inexpensive student violins. These strings come with a black tube on each string, and a built in surprise, whether for the installer or the student. These tubes are apparently extremely slippery, and if the bridge angle is slightly off the equilibrium value, and if the feet of the bridge are not exactly fitted to correspond to this, the bridge will soon crash down onto the front of the instrument with a loud startling "WHAP" sound. The obvious and apparently essential solution is to remove 2 or 3 of these (that on the E-string is retained), thus providing enough friction to retain one's sanity.

This fingerboard removal (and attachment) thread has been useful and interesting. In my business I provide lots of student and better cellos. The better ones, regardless of source, generally have correct and trouble-free fingerboards. But it seems in the "student" range (usually the price range with lacquer instead of varnish) even though the ebony and maple are of high quality, there are a variety of fingerboard problems. Some of these have been mentioned. The "bump" you mentioned . . . is one. Generally there are frequent buzz problems, requiring both initial and subsequent planing. The boards are likely to have a variety of bumps and a general tendency toward longitudinal convexity instead of the required concavity. Some of the reasons for this may be:
- poor fingerboard manufacturing control (ideally they are milled with the correct surface from seasoned ebony)
- poor or no corrective planing at setup
- cellos shipped with strings pulled down against board, warping it
- cellos stacked together in bags, warping it down
- green ebony warping as it seasons (statistically this should go up or down, but usually the lower end droops rather than rises this)
- low string action at the bridge end developing after a time (probably from longitudinal shrinkage of the green flamed back maple as it seasons; 4 mm change is not unusual, and sometimes an abnormally high bridge becomes needed)
Once these cellos have been fully seasoned and correctly planed they may be quite stable and satisfactory for the duration, but in the meantime teachers and all must be on the alert lest these problems discourage the student unaware. It seems one cannot rely on the highly competitive manufacturers and suppliers of such instruments to dry their wood, and it's best to buy them a year ahead of use. Much of this is from a learning cycle as well as cost delivery pressures in these newer factories. You will not generally find such problems in older factories in Germany and the Czech Republic that operate from stocks of well seasoned wood - no matter how much shiny lacquer they apply ;-) But all things considered, it is not practical to ignore the advantages of the new crop of vastly improved and impressively priced (to say the least) instruments from new sources in China and elsewhere.

Finally found the leisure moment this evening to read the current Strings Magazine, highly enjoyed the article by our Carl Applebaum recounting his outreach expedition to Cuba and Luthiers sin Fronteras program to provide working instruments and badly needed string repair facilities there. Highly recommended to your reading, perhaps even contribution. You will recall Carl's discussion here of plans for this before it happened. Paul Jacobs was a major contributor as well as several other members mentioned in the article. Nice to get some good news like this.

Speaking of apples and bananas, the letters to the editor in this same issue of Strings were significant and gratifying, in particular those on the unpleasant business of teacher commissions. That by past president of the VSA, Eric Chapman, was particularly telling. Nice to see this aired in such an open forum.

My son, Henry Jr, made his first violin with a slab-cut back from my favorite "Sweet Home" log. It has a wonderful warm and easy playing sound. He had not tried to sell it, but a visitor from Nashville last month paid Henry's quickly improvised price of $3k on the spot. (You can see Henry varnishing this violin at: www.henrystrobel.com/violvar.htm)
Instruments from this log have always been wonderful. It is beautifully very deeply curled, hence not stiff. It also was perhaps standing dead for a bit and lay for a while before sawing up. So not white, and perhaps affected to a degree by "fungus." But, as I have always maintained, stiffness is not an absolute figure of merit in maple, and I like to suppose that this log has the right properties of low frequency low damping and high frequency loss. But I have no particular interest in performing tests on it, which, in this business, usually seem to provide ambivalent results. Ah, the art of the violin maker.

I used to do this, but have not for years. I used a Paasche airbrush. The technique can be used to blend over repairs where the original varnish has been feather sanded away, as on a previously botched school bass neck repair, using thinned spirit varnish colored with aniline dye. Nowadays I generally use a glaze in such cases. In Violin Making, Step by Step, page 72, I described the process for spray varnishing a new violin to get away from the difficulties of brushing. The result can be quick and good. (Karl Roy complimented me on one of these varnish jobs, but I think he didn't know how it was done. ;-) Here's the relevant paragraph: "[Or completely eliminate the problem by spraying it with an air brush. In spraying spirit varnish, one can put essentially all the color "coats" on in one session. Level any "orange peel"on the surface by wet sanding the still thick and tender varnish the next day. Watch out for fingerprints, etc. French polish it. In a few weeks the varnish will have hardened and shrunk down onto the wood like a thin skin. There are indeed many ways to varnish.]"

You will see many fingerboards with broad pits in them, not just string furrows or fingernail marks. These are simply from the fingertips. Many good violinists really "hammer " the board, and if it is not periodically planed, you will see these. It's a sign of use, lots of use.

2003

I have used many of the Gewa (Güth) "resonators" in cellos with good results. These are apparently higher Q devices than those described by von Reumont, and which I have not tried. But they are not just weights. He indicates that their action depends on the phase shift from the combined mounting material of felt and rubber cement.

(For viola) 1/4 is a relatively unusual size, but out of the hundreds of starter outfits each year we do several. Some of the 4th graders will play viola, whether by choice or assignment, and some will be too small for the normal 4th grade size of 1/2. (These sizes correspond to the violin sizes from which they are adapted.) I don't remember all the various C strings we have ended up with, but I do know we spend some time experimenting typically, depending on what strings are on hand, and the peculiarities of the box. I do recall that the . . . strings we tried for this are pretty dismal (fuzzy sounding). Sometimes longer strings cut down seem better than the specified small thick ones. We do use lots of Preludes on the small fiddles for economic reasons . . .No, I don't think going an octave higher would satisfy most school teachers. I would be pleased to hear any silver bullet recommendations for this. . . . Yes, apart from the tone difficulty with the small thick strings there is the practical problem of installing and tuning them. The bulk in the pegbox is one problem, as is the difficulty of fitting them into either integral tailpiece tuners or the "on the string" type tuners.

❧

(About cycloids) It's also interesting that Mersenne, who had earlier derived the basic string vibrating equation, first (I think) defined the general cycloid. PS A number of such curves are treated in this reference I cited in my Art & Method of the Violin Maker, 1992. Footnote 8. Tullio Pigoli surveys a number of these in La Tracciatura, Quaderni di Liuteria No. 4, Gruppo Studi Liutari, Cremona n.d. Of course the medieval architects (and carpenters) drew non circular arcs. They knew how to use various sliding trammels, the pencil guided by a string fixed at two points (to draw an ellipse), or unwinding from a spool (to draw the spiral of Vignola), etc. The reader may find it interesting to try these pencil and string techniques. While our general approach is from the obvious compass and rule position, the violin maker is (and was) certainly not necessarily limited to these. We might also mention the proportional (double-ended) compass; while this could be used for, say, the golden section, more likely this ratio resulted from the 2:1 triangular construction. I just dug up the Cremona textbook I had referred to below. It includes large drawings for, among other things, a "metodo per tracciare le quinte della tavola e del fondo del violino (T. Pigoli) col metodo dell' ipocicloide (A) e della concoide della retta (B) and "metodo per tracciare le seste della tavola e del fondo del violino (T. Pigoli) col metodo della sezione dell' ipocicloide. I can translate if anyone doesn't read Italian.

For those with a windows computer, one way to print ccycloid curves output from that program in ps is to download Ghostscript. With that I was able to print tiled 8.5x11 in sheets on my PCL laserjet. I had suggested Ghostscript as a workaround for those who do not have the more expensive full Acrobat (and thus Distiller), doubtless a majority. Ghostscript, and the related GSViewer, make up the poor man's free postscript interpreter. (You do need to be a little nerdy, and if I can qualify, I guess most here can. ;-)

❧

Thanks for reminding me. Dr. Muratov now lives and works in Australia. Seven years ago Vladimir Baginsky . . . sent me Muratov's earlier book in Russian, which I cited in Art & Method of the Violin Maker.. Dr. Muratov had recently emailed me about this new book, and I had been meaning to get it but did not until you reminded me. I downloaded it as a pdf from 1st Books Library (the URL you gave below) for $3.95, about 11M in size. It represents a very large endeavor, and is definitely worth it just to flip through, admiring the geometrical drawings. You can also buy the paperback for $11.95. He uses clothoids. ("Different strokes for different folks." ;-). Very comprehensive and lots of fitting to classical violins. The latest example of how countless different geometric schemes can be used to generate violins. I guess the important thing in all this geometrical "analysis" is to try to find what methods are of value to us, and if possible to understand which methods were used in the past. Certainly circular arcs, and maybe cycloids! Not explicitly, but beginning on page 110 he shows how to proceed with compass and straightedge and a "springy string" held at both ends. Think of using a piece of purfling and tracing the curve from it. Well, I have to get some work done now. Having looked a few minutes more at Muratov's book, I think the text is very interesting too. Of course he does not claim that the old luthiers used this spiral explicitly in violin design. (It is used by ship, roller coaster, and highway designers.)

Well, I didn't think this would be a tough question. Whoever coined this apparently recent word would know. . . Could it actually mean cloth-like, as conchoid means conchlike? I'm not a mathematician. Please excuse me for interrupting a serious discussion with a whimsical question. I am an habitual etymologist, and, noting the words silk, canvas, and stockinet that just came up in connection with cloth-oid, I thought "Oh . . ?" But seriously, can anyone tell me the etymology (presumably Greek) of clothoid; I can't find it in any dictionary. Well, back to work.

❧

When doing a forced vibration of a bass or cello as in a "vibration dedamping" experiment, there is a very strong alternating "breeze" at the soundhole, not surprising when the edge of the hole is pumping in and out with an amplitude of several mm, as seen with a stroboscope. Indeed this is not a rigid Helmholtz resonator.

❧

(In a discussion of what luthiers see over their workbenches) I have a window looking into my grape arbor. On the other hand, a customer recently looked out my "store" window and saw half a dozen long-horn cattle where they oughtn't be. My neighbor had left and left a gate open. So I had to leave her and round up a couple of other neighbors. Maybe not inspiring, but stimulating.

USEFUL MEASUREMENTS FOR VIOLIN MAKERS
by Henry Strobel

(This classic, essential handbook is the standard reference for size and adjustment of violin family instruments.)

PREFACES 5
Frontispiece 8

Chapter 1. STANDARD SIZE INSTRUMENTS
Introduction 9
Table of Useful Measurements 10
Remarks on the Table 11
Bridge and Fingerboard Templates 12
Bow Measurements 13

Chapter 2. OTHER INSTRUMENT SIZES
Introduction 14
Table of Violin Sizes 16
Table of Viola Sizes 16
Table of Cello Sizes 17
Table of Bass Sizes 17
Bridge Templates for Small Instruments 18

Chapter 3. NOTES ON VARIOUS SUBJECTS
Introduction 19
Tuning 19
Strings 19
The Bridge 21
Standard Violin Diagram 22
Standard Cello Diagram 22
The Sound Post 23
Measuring the Post Position 23
The Bass Bar 24
Wolf Tones 24
The Double Bass 24
Common Fiddle Faults 25
Factory Fiddles 25
Plywood Cellos and Basses 25

Chapter 4. SOME HISTORICAL AND OTHER BOWED INSTRUMENTS
The Baroque Violin 26
Viola d'Amore 27
The Viol Family 27
Historical Note 28
The New Violin "Octet" 28
Miscellaneous Others 29

Chapter 5. FURTHER REFERENCE
Introduction 31
Bibliography 31
Periodicals 33
"Term Translator" 33
Violinist's "Notes" 37

Chapter 6. MAKER'S ADDENDUM
Introduction 38
Measuring Tools 38
Table of Additional Measurements 40
Graduation 41
Varnish 42
Wood 42
Glue 43
Graduation Control 43

AFTERWORD
Making and Repair 44
New and Old 45
About the Author 45
Notes 46
Tables of Typical Body Sizes 47
Basic Care of String Instruments (For Students) 47

VIOLIN MAKER'S NOTEBOOK
by Henry Strobel

(A shop reference manual. Illustrated procedures, etc.)

PREFACE 5
BOW REHAIRING & MINOR BOW REPAIRS
Introduction 7
Materials 7
Overview 9
Tools for Rehairing 10
Bow Rehairing Fixture 11
Nomenclature of the Bow 12
Rehairing Procedure 12
Examination 12
Disassembly 13
Repairs 15
Reassembly (Rehairing) 15
Reexamination 18
Some Routine Bow Repairs 19
Glues Used in Bow Work 19
Cleaning and Polishing 20
Springing or Straightening 20
Broken Head 20
Replacing The Ivory Tip 21
Worn Stick 21
Broken Stick 21
Bent Ferrule 21
Replacing The Slide 22
Replacing A Pearl Eye 22
Loose Underslide 22
Chipped Frog 22
Cracked Frog 22
Replacing The Eyelet 22
Replacing The Button 23
Silver Wrapping 23
"Whalebone" Wrapping 25
Leather Grip 25
Adjusting Balance or Weight 25
Further Reading 26
CRACK AND VARNISH REPAIRS
Introduction 27
Crack Repair 27
Crack Cleaning 27
Crack Gluing 29
Crack Reinforcement 30
Crack Filling 30
Varnish Restoration 31
Violin Varnish 31
Retouching Varnish 31
Color Matching 32
"Spirits" and "Oils" 35
Cleaning and Polishing 35
Introduction 35
Cleaning 36
Polishing 36
Further Reading 38
SAFETY AND HEALTH
Introduction 40
Inhalation Hazards 40
Contact Hazards 42
Ingestion Hazards 42
Fire Hazards 42
Other Hazards 43
PHOTOGRAPHING VIOLINS
Introduction 44
Assumptions 44
Camera Selection And Operation 45
Equipment Arrangement 46
Background 46
Instrument Support 46
Lights 47
Camera Support 47
Lighting Adjustment 47

Reference 49
"Photogenic Fiddles" 50
INTERVALS AND TUNING
Introduction and Definitions 52
Just Major Scale 52
Circle of Fifths 53
Chromatic Scale 53
Table of Intervals 55
Keys 55
Pitch and Frequency 56
Instrument Ranges 56
Temperament and the Violinist 57
Further Reading 57
THE CONNOISSEUR
Introduction 58
Classes of Violins 59
Guidelines 60
Further Reading 61
Auction Prices 61
Reference Information 61
Miscellany 65
APPENDIX - A REPAIR EXAMPLE "Wherein a Valued Violin,
Grievously Damaged in a Car Crash, is returned to Health." 67
What Happened 67
Collect, Study, and Store the Pieces 67
Reconstruct the Front 67
Inlay a Sound Post Patch 68
Retouch the Front Cracks 71
Remove the Button from the Neck 71
Reattach and Reinforce the Button 71
Graft the Neck 72
Repair the Fingerboard 73
Reset the Neck 73
Glue the Front on 73
Setup and Adjust 73

⋙

HEALTH OF THE VIOLIN, VIOLA, CELLO
by Lucien Greilsamer
Translated from the French by Henry Strobel

"Practical Advice on the Acquisition, Maintenance, Adjustment,
and Conservation of Bowed Instruments"

(The first appearance in English of this classic from 1910.)

CHAPTER I - General "Health": Conditions in Which an
Instrument Should Always be Kept to Maintain its Good
Qualities 7

CHAPTER II - THE STRINGS: THEORY OF FITTING UP;
TABLE OF OPTIMUM PRACTICAL GAUGES 10

CHAPTER III - THE STOP: DIFFERENT METHODS OF
DETERMINING AND CHECKING IT. TABLE OF OPTIMUM
MEASUREMENTS 13

CHAPTER IV - THE FINGERBOARD PROJECTION AND ITS
CONSEQUENCES: HEIGHT OF THE STRINGS OVER THE
FINGERBOARD; THEIR ANGLE OVER THE BRIDGE.
DIMENSIONS OF THE BRIDGE 14

Chapter V - The Bar and the Post 16

CHAPTER VI - ABOUT AN INTERNATIONAL VIOLIN MAKING
COMPETITION. WHO IS THE BEST JUDGE? 18

CHAPTER VII - CERTAIN SIGNS OF EXCELLENCE IN AN
INSTRUMENT 20

CHAPTER VIII - SHORTCUTS: BAKING THE WOOD,

STAINING WITH BICHROMATE 22

CHAPTER IX - NECESSARY PRECAUTIONS IN
PURCHASING AN ANTIQUE 23

CHAPTER X - CRACKS AND REPAIRS 26

CHAPTER XI - SOME USEFUL RECOMMENDATIONS FOR
THE MAINTENANCE AND CONSERVATION OF BOWED
INSTRUMENTS 30

THE VARIOUS PARTS OF A BOWED INSTRUMENT.
NOMENCLATURE AND DEFINITIONS 31

PRINCIPAL TERMS USED IN VIOLIN MAKING 34

WORKS ON VIOLIN MAKING WORTH CONSULTING . . . 36

⋙

ART & METHOD OF THE VIOLIN MAKER
by Henry Strobel

(Notes on the design, and background of the violin. Continuing
education for violin makers.)

(Addendum to 2nd Ed . . . . Inside Front Cover)
Preface to the Second Edition 4
Preface to the First Edition 5
THE SHAPE OF THE VIOLIN 7
Introduction 7
A Lute and a Viol 9
ANALYSIS OF A VIOLIN OUTLINE 10
TRADITIONAL PROPORTIONS 10
GOLDEN DIVISION OF THE BODY . . . 11
A "RATIONALIZED" DESIGN 13
A SECOND LOOK 15
THE OUTLINE OF THE SCROLL 19
PERSPECTIVE AND OPINION 25
THE MOLD 27
MOLD OUTLINE 27
MOLD TYPES 28
THE NON-MOLD 28
BUILT ON THE BACK 28
BUILT ON A BOARD 29
BUILT "ON THE TABLE" 29
THE OUTSIDE MOLD 30
THE INSIDE MOLD 30
THE ASSEMBLY PROCESS 30
THE BLOCKS 32
THE WOOD 36
SELECTION OF THE WOOD 36
SPECIES 36
MAIN BODY WOODS 36
OTHER WOODS 37
GRAIN 38
FIGURE 38
CUTTING THE WOOD 41
GRAIN ORIENTATION 42

THE RIBS 44
HEIGHT TAPER 44
SURFACE CROWN 45
CORNER CONTROL 45
CORNER OVERHANG 46
TABLE AND BACK 48
JOINING THE TWO PIECES 48
CUTTING THEM OUT 48
ARCHING 49
"ARCH-TYPES" 49
PURFLING 50
GRADUATION 52

BACK GRADUATION 53
TABLE GRADUATION 53
REGRADUATION 53
THEORY AND PRACTICE 54
THE *f*'S 56
THE BAR 56
REBARRING 57
SPRINGING THE BAR 57
AN OBSERVATION 57
ATTACHING THE BACK 58
"PUTTING THE LID ON IT" 58
AESTHETIC OBSERVATIONS 60
SCULPTURE & THE ARTIST'S EYE 60
CURVES OF GRACE 60
BALANCE AND TRANSITION 61
EDGEWORK 61
FITTINGS 62
THE NECK 64
"GETTING A HANDLE ON IT" 64
THE ANTIQUE NECK 64
A CURIOUS OLD VIOLIN 65
THE MORTISED NECK 66
THE GRAFTED NECK 66
NECK REPAIR: A PRACTICAL
DIGRESSION 68
RULES 68
PROCEDURES 68
NECK BROKEN AT HEEL . . 68
NECK BROKEN AT PEGBOX 69
NECK RESETTING 69
VARNISHING 71
FITTING UP: SOME PRACTICAL DIGRESSIONS 73
POSTS 73
PEGS 73
BRIDGES 74
The Author (Photograph) 76
INDEX 77
(Addendum to 1st Ed. . . . . Inside Back Cover)

ð

VIOLIN MAKING, STEP BY STEP
by Henry Strobel

(Clear, Comprehensive, fundamental Method)

PREFACE 5
PRELIMINARY 7
BEFORE STARTING 7
TOOLS AND PROCEDURES 7
OTHER READING 8
OUR WORK SPACE 8
PRINCIPLES OF CUTTING TOOLS 10
SHARPENING EDGED TOOLS 10
THE RIGHT GLUE 14
THE MODEL AND PATTERNS 15
THE MODEL 16
THE PATTERNS 16
THE MOLD 18
BEFORE STARTING 18
LAYING IT OUT 18
CUTTING IT OUT 18
PREPARING THE BLOCKS 19
GLUING THE BLOCKS 19
LEVELING THE BLOCKS 19
MARKING THE BLOCKS 19
SHAPING THE BLOCKS 19
THE RIBS 21
BEFORE STARTING 21
CUTTING OUT THE RIBS 21
THICKNESSING THE RIBS 21
SELECTING THE RIBS 21

THE BENDING PROCESS 21
THE MIDDLE RIBS 22
THE UPPER RIBS 23
THE LOWER RIBS 23
TAPERING THE RIBS 23
CUTTING THE LININGS 24
INSTALLING THE LININGS 24
FINISHING THE RIBS OUTSIDE 24
THE BACK 25
BEFORE STARTING 25
THE BACK WOOD 25
JOINING THE BACK 25
TRACING THE BACK OUTLINE 26
CUTTING OUT THE BACK 26
THE CRADLE 27
PRELIMINARY ARCHING 27
THE PURFLING 28
THE FINAL ARCHING 31
HOLLOWING THE BACK 33
GRADUATING THE BACK 34
ABOUT TAP TONES 36
THE FRONT 37
THE FRONT WOOD 37
JOINING THE FRONT 37
TRACING THE OUTLINE 37
CUTTING OUT THE FRONT 37
PRELIMINARY ARCHING 37
PURFLING 37
FINAL ARCHING 37
HOLLOWING THE FRONT 38
MARKING THE SOUND HOLES 38
FULL SIZE DRAWINGS 39
TABLE OF MEASUREMENTS 42
THE FRONT (CONTINUED) 43
CUTTING THE SOUND HOLES 44
GRADUATING THE FRONT 45
BARRING 45
THE BODY 48
REMOVING THE MOLD 48
FINISHING THE INSIDE 49
GLUING THE BACK ON 49
THE LABEL 49
GLUING THE FRONT ON 50
THE SADDLE 50
THE EDGES 51
THE NECK & SCROLL 52
CUTTING IT OUT 53
HOLLOWING THE PEGBOX 54
CARVING THE VOLUTE 54
THE FINGERBOARD 57
THE NUT 59
ATTACHING THE NECK 59
FINISHING THE NECK 60
FITTING UP 62
THE PEGS 62
THE ENDBUTTON 64
THE POST 64
THE STRINGS 65
THE TAILPIECE 65
THE BRIDGE 66
TESTING 70
VARNISHING 71
BEFORE STARTING 71
THE VARNISH PROPER 73
POLISHING 75
SUMMARY OF VARNISHING STEPS 76
FINAL FITTINGS 77

ð

VIOLA MAKING, STEP BY STEP
by Henry Strobel

((For use with Violin Making, Step by Step, which it refers to)

PREFACE TO THE FIRST EDITION 5

PRELIMINARY 7
    BEFORE STARTING 7
    KEY REFERENCES 7
    BACKGROUND READING 8

THE MODEL AND PATTERNS 9
    ABOUT SIZES 9
    THE PATTERNS 9
    "SMALL" DEMONSTRATION MODEL 10
    "LARGE" AND OTHER MODELS 12
    "MEDIUM" MODELS 13

TABLE OF VIOLA MEASUREMENTS 16

FULL SIZE DRAWINGS, "SMALL" VIOLA 17-20

THE MODEL AND PATTERNS (CONTINUED) 21

THE MOLD 24
    BEFORE STARTING 24
    LAYING IT OUT 24
    CUTTING IT OUT 24
    PREPARING THE BLOCKS 24
    GLUING THE BLOCKS 24
    LEVELING THE BLOCKS 24
    MARKING THE BLOCKS 24
    SHAPING THE BLOCKS 24

THE RIBS 25
    BEFORE STARTING 25
    CUTTING OUT THE RIBS 25
    THICKNESSING THE RIBS 25
    SELECTING THE RIBS 25
    THE BENDING PROCESS 25
    THE MIDDLE RIBS 25
    THE UPPER RIBS 25
    THE LOWER RIBS 25
    TAPERING THE RIBS 25
    CUTTING THE LININGS 25
    INSTALLING THE LININGS 25
    FINISHING THE RIBS OUTSIDE 25

THE BACK 26
    BEFORE STARTING 26
    THE BACK WOOD 26
    JOINING THE BACK 26
    POWER TOOL NOTES 26
    TRACING THE BACK OUTLINE 26
    CUTTING OUT THE BACK 26
    ARCHING CONTOUR GUIDES 26
    THE CRADLE 26
    PRELIMINARY ARCHING 26
    THE PURFLING 26
    THE FINAL ARCHING 27
    HOLLOWING THE BACK 27
    GRADUATING THE BACK 27
    TAP TONES 27
    OPTIONAL ASSEMBLY SEQUENCE 27

THE FRONT 28
    THE FRONT WOOD 28
    JOINING THE FRONT 28
    TRACING THE OUTLINE 28
    CUTTING OUT THE FRONT 28
    PRELIMINARY ARCHING 28
    PURFLING 28
    FINAL ARCHING 28

HOLLOWING THE FRONT 28
MARKING THE SOUND HOLES 28
CUTTING THE SOUND HOLES 28
GRADUATING THE FRONT 28
BARRING 29

THE BODY 30
    REMOVING THE MOLD 30
    FINISHING THE INSIDE 30
    GLUING THE BACK ON 30
    THE LABEL 30
    GLUING THE FRONT ON 30
    THE SADDLE 30
    THE EDGES 30

THE NECK & SCROLL 31
    CUTTING IT OUT 31
    HOLLOWING THE PEGBOX 31
    CARVING THE VOLUTE 31
    THE FINGERBOARD 31
    FINGERBOARD STABILITY 31
    THE NUT 31
    ATTACHING THE NECK 31
    FINISHING THE NECK 31

FITTING UP 33
    THE PEGS 33
    THE ENDPIN 33
    THE POST 33

THE STRINGS 33
    THE TAILPIECE 33
    THE BRIDGE 33

VARNISHING, ETC. 33

AFTERWORD 34
FRONT OF EARLY STRADIVARI VIOLA . . . . Endpapers

CELLO MAKING, STEP BY STEP
by Henry Strobel

(For use with Violin Making, Step by Step, which it refers to)

PREFACE TO THE THIRD EDITION 2
PREFACE TO THE FIRST EDITION 5
PRELIMINARY 7
    BEFORE STARTING 7
    KEY REFERENCES 7
    A WORD ABOUT WOOD 8
THE MODEL AND PATTERNS 9
THE MOLD 10
    BEFORE STARTING 10
    LAYING IT OUT 10
    CUTTING IT OUT 10
        FRONT & BACK LAYERS 10
        MIDDLE "LAYER" 11
    PREPARING THE BLOCKS 12
    GLUING THE BLOCKS 12
    LEVELING THE BLOCKS 12
    MARKING THE BLOCKS 12
    SHAPING THE BLOCKS 12
THE RIBS 13
    BEFORE STARTING 13
    CUTTING OUT THE RIBS 13
    THICKNESSING THE RIBS 13
    SELECTING THE RIBS 13
    THE BENDING PROCESS 13
    THE RIB CLAMPS 13
    THE MIDDLE RIBS 14

THE UPPER RIBS 14
THE LOWER RIBS 14
TAPERING THE RIBS 14
CUTTING THE LININGS 15
INSTALLING THE LININGS 15
FINISHING THE RIBS OUTSIDE 15
THE BACK 16
BEFORE STARTING 16
THE BACK WOOD 16
JOINING THE BACK 16
POWER TOOL NOTES 17
TRACING THE BACK OUTLINE 17
CUTTING OUT THE BACK 17
ARCHING CONTOUR GUIDES 18
THE CRADLE 19
PRELIMINARY ARCHING 20
BULK WOOD REMOVAL NOTES 20
THE OVERHEAD ROUTER METHOD 22
SMOOTHING THE ARCHING 23
THE PURFLING 23
TABLE OF CELLO MEASUREMENTS 24
FULL SIZE DRAWINGS, 4/4 CELLO 25

(Addendum for 7/8 Size Cello Inserted Here, A1-A12)

THE BACK, CONTINUED 41
THE FINAL ARCHING 41
HOLLOWING THE BACK 43
GRADUATING THE BACK 45
TAP TONES 45
OPTIONAL ASSEMBLY SEQUENCE 46
THE FRONT 47
THE FRONT WOOD 47
JOINING THE FRONT 47
TRACING THE OUTLINE 47
CUTTING OUT THE FRONT 47
PRELIMINARY ARCHING 47
PURFLING 47
FINAL ARCHING 47
HOLLOWING THE FRONT 47
MARKING THE SOUND HOLES 47
CUTTING THE SOUND HOLES 48
GRADUATING THE FRONT 49
BARRING 49
THE BODY 51
REMOVING THE MOLD 51
FINISHING THE INSIDE 51
GLUING THE BACK ON 52
THE LABEL 52
GLUING THE FRONT ON 52
THE SADDLE 52
THE EDGES 52
THE NECK & SCROLL 53
CUTTING IT OUT 54
HOLLOWING THE PEGBOX 55
CARVING THE VOLUTE 55
THE FINGERBOARD 55
FINGERBOARD STABILITY 56
THE NUT 56
ATTACHING THE NECK 56
FINISHING THE NECK 56
FITTING UP 57
THE PEGS 57
THE ENDPIN 57
THE POST 58
THE STRINGS 58
THE TAILPIECE 58
THE BRIDGE 58
TESTING 60
VARNISHING AND ADJUSTMENT 61
AFTERWORD 62

ADDENDUM FOR A 7/8 SIZE CELLO

Violin Making - *Live!* or "*Watch Me Make a Cello, Step by Step,*" is Henry Strobel's first video. In it he demonstrates and explains the violin maker's procedures and processes (common to violin, viola, and cello), using a cello as the example. Fortunately the cello model adapted a 7/8 size J. B. Guadagnini made a wonderful sounding instrument in a size just right for a neglected minority of cellists. The documentation to reproduce it, lacking in the video, is published as an addendum to this Third Edition of *Cello Making, Step by Step* at the *center of the book*, just above the 4/4 size drawings. Readily removable for use, its pages are numbered A1 through A12, leaving the pagination of the basic book unchanged for reference reasons.

A1	Table of 7/8 Size Cello Metric Measurements
A2	Lower Neck Pattern & Misc. Notes
A4 & A9	Lower Half of Body Drawing
A6 & A7	Upper Half of Body Drawing (center of book)
A11	Scroll Pattern & Transverse Arching Guides
A12	Pine Resin - Walnut Oil Varnish Recipe
Back Cover	Full size profile photo of the scroll.

~

VIDEO: "*Watch Me Make a Cello, Step by Step*" by Henry Strobel

This video is a set of 3 VHS SP cassettes, NTSC or PAL, running almost six hours. It can supplement the "Step by Step" books for violin, viola or cello, but is also an independent educational resource for anyone interested in the practical procedures and artistic processes of the violin maker, which are described and demonstrated close-up and in detail by Henry Strobel in his workshop. Makers and would-be makers will be interested in practically every scene; others will want to fast-forward in areas, but will find much of interest.

As in his books, Mr. Strobel has a personal, but clear presentation. In addition to the traditional procedures he includes some innovative or alternative ones, equally professional. (See the book, Cello Making, Step by Step, above. Full size drawings and measurements for the 7/8 "Guadagnini" cello, varnish information, etc., have been added to complement the video.) Please note: The general procedures of the violin maker are shown in this video using a cello as an example - they are similar for the violin, viola and cello

REFLECTIONS (PERSONAL ESSAYS)
by Henry A. Strobel

(This is a personal, non-technical book, but it may be of interest to some friends, colleagues, and students. Beautifully typeset and printed, illustrated, hard bound, in a first edition of 500 numbered copies. For those who will understandably not buy it, here is a sample chapter.)

FOREWORD 4
Chapter 1. GROWING UP IN INDIANA 7
Chapter 2. MY CONTINUING EDUCATION 13
Chapter 3. AN ENGINEER IN CALIFORNIA 18
Chapter 4. VIOLIN MAKER & PUBLISHER IN OREGON 25
Chapter 5. MAN THE WORKER, MAN THE ARTIST 33
Chapter 6. SIMPLE PLEASURES, QUIET TREASURES 39
Chapter 7. THE TRUE AND THE GOOD 85
ANNUAL LETTERS 103
FAMILY ALBUM 120
AFTERWORD 12

Sample Chapter 4. VIOLIN MAKER & PUBLISHER IN OREGON

My mid-life change of career had early roots. About the fourth grade I had read a book in the public library, a saccharine story of the life of Mathias Klotz, the proto-typical violin maker of Mittenwald, and at that age it impressed and inspired me. I also studied the violin in elementary school and picked it up again from time to time thereafter. When I left Scotland, I brought a violin with me. Not a very good one, and it inspired me to make my own. Working in Palo Alto in 1966 I had found the violin shop of Leon LaFosse, who provided me with tools, Hungarian maple, German spruce, and unfailing encouragement. My principal distraction from engineering in those days (apart from young ladies, sailboats, and such) was learning violin making. I read everything I could find on it and got to know most of the violin makers in the area, imbibing the elixir of arcane information at every opportunity. In each house I lived, in San Francisco, Fairfax, and Novato, priority was given to the workshop. I came to have a double life — although a full-time engineer I also had a commercial violin repair business, first registered in California in 1978. I had made several violins, but I knew I would learn the most from examining and repairing many instruments, and this I have continued to do. The great thing here is to be aware of one's limitations and responsibilities for the property of others and the heritage of the past. I have always been strictly conscientious to "First, do no harm."

Since I was essentially educating myself in this craft, this art, I put a lot of effort into compiling measurement and adjustment data for the bowed instruments — violin, viola, cello, bass, in all sizes. I studied, compared, and analyzed this information by direct measurement of instruments in my shop and in music stores, from the available literature, and from notes gathered through the grapevine from respected violin shops and the professional violin making schools. I knew I needed to know this stuff! Eventually this coalesced into a small book called *Useful Measurements for Violin Makers*, which I completed and published in Oregon in 1988. I devised the symbol of the calipers and violin for the cover of that book, and it remains my publishing trademark, as on this book.

The plan was to move to Oregon and build a country house of our own. We had explored here some years before and so in early 1985 I came again, empowered by Susan and the children to find the right place. When I found it I knew it, just as when I had met Susan. Such a beautiful place, but there was already a (one layer) house on it. Fine, said I, we will live in the first storey while we add the second. I meticulously measured the house, and by the time the loose ends were tied up in Novato I had bought the place and drawn the plans. We moved in; I hired a congenial, competent carpenter and we carpentered. Wary of rain, we first built the upper walls and the second roof. Only then did we cut up the old roof and defenestrate it piece-wise. This time the library (where I sit typing now) took first priority, looking out over Mill Creek in the back yard. Gradually the violin shop areas were expanded, along with the business.

Exacting, repetitive work, but there are compensations, and the atmosphere of the violin workshop is pleasant to proprietor and visitor alike. Good violins are magical, agile, functional sculpture. The visiting artist plies them with Mozart, Bach, or Bruch to the accompaniment, next door, of plane and gouge shaping and fitting the flexible, figured maple, the simple, straightforward spruce - soon to be married by the glue of beasts, anointed with the oil of walnut and lavender, colored with madder and earth of Sienna, tensioned with the inner strings of sheep, stroked with the tail of a Siberian stallion, and so to sing.

The right wood (with the right work) makes the violin, and a violin maker could hardly choose a more fortunate place than Oregon. Fine Engelmann and Sitka spruce are here and maple in abundance, although a lot of the Oregon maple has a homely look from its rapid rainy growth. It was my great good fortune to find a log of singular, exquisitely figured, acoustically superb maple. A logger, son-in-law of a local cellist friend had cut a tree several years earlier of the most beautiful, broadly, deeply "flamed" maple, four feet thick. It had grown slowly at a high altitude and was already nearly seasoned. I bought several cello length sections of this log, cut them into wedges on a "head rig" (saw mill), and still have a good reserve of it in our barn loft. This is my "holy" wood, which makes glorious sounding instruments - in spite of my best efforts. Only God can make a tree - at least such a tree. My logger friend's mother-in-law bought and played the first cello I made of that wood and her daughter, also a professional cellist, now plays it.

So what does it mean to be a violin maker? Like a shoemaker or watchmaker, it doesn't usually mean you only *make* them. In my violin shop, like most, a lot of the work involves repairing and adjusting instruments for optimum tone and ease of playing. They are fickle, fragile things made of wood and animal glue, affected by weather, use, and abuse. They must sound their best and not pose unnecessary obstacles for the student or get in the way of the performer. This work seems simple, but requires years of experience, even a gift, a vocation, to do well. Simply making a violin is a fairly trivial task; most anyone can, and it will doubtless sound like a violin. This is the level readily attained by the amateur maker, who deservedly derives satisfaction from making with